Teach Like It's The Zombie Apocalypse

Woody Underwood

Dedication

To Elizabeth, Carson, and Emma Underwood. The best "zombie slayers" and alliance members I could ever have.

Also…

To anyone who has or will have an "educational zombie apocalypse", stay encouraged and positive in your daily "battles"!

Table of Contents

-Preface-

One of my greatest passions in life is teaching and leading young people. I don't know a greater reward than seeing a child finally "get" a concept and knowing I played a vital role in that process. Seeing the fruits of a lesson that was created and presented is truly a blessing beyond measure. I am sure that you, like I, have had similar experiences in your career.

Education, like other professions, has many barriers that we must address and overcome on a daily basis. As a result of the many issues I have seen teachers face; I have felt a heavy burden to reach out and hopefully encourage those who may be going through what I refer to as an educational zombie apocalypse.

I would like to start by saying the insights for this book have been gained through personal experience, sitting through church services, listening to teachers as well as other educational professionals, and working with students. In no way is this book intended to offend any particular group of people. It simply looks at the parallels that exist between those brutal days of educational survival and what would occur during a zombie apocalypse.

Before we delve too deep in this comparison it may be wise to do a quick description of what an actual zombie apocalypse would look like. Most zombie movies and books all have the same basic storyline. At some point in history, a new virus strand has been discovered. That virus impacts a few unlucky souls, causing them to eventually die, well "sort of die". You see the virus allows for the human to undergo a mutation that essentially changes the infected through death to a walking corpse. The dead now rises, walks, and seeks out new "healthy" hosts to infect by biting them. Once a new victim is bitten, they are infected and experience a quick death. Upon death, the corpse changes and begins to "turn" as the virus flows through their body. At this point, the zombie population starts to rapidly increase. The undead is nearly indestructible unless you strike a vital blow to their brain. Attacking the brain is the only way to defeat a zombie. During this time of mass chaos you have people fleeing, seeking shelter, learning to fight in new ways, and discovering there are even greater enemies in the world (fellow living humans). The mindsets of people start to change, small groups and alliances begin forming.

Relationships are built because the need to work together is critical if you wish to survive. The world can seem very bleak and desolate but there is no time to complain or feel sorry for yourself. Your only goal is to survive the current day and work on restoring the world to its former status by searching for a cure to this deadly virus.

For those who believe what I just described will actually happen in the future, although I feel/hope that number is very low, I would respectfully disagree with you. Even though I don't think humans will undergo some massive biological change that converts us into nearly indestructible, mindless beings, I admit that I enjoy reading, writing, and watching a variety of science fiction. In that genre of science fiction I have grown not just attached to zombies, but the PROBLEMS that would come from having a zombie mutiny.

I believe that many of the problems we face as educators have a direct correlation to an undead uprising. As you read, you will see those correlations and how I apply them to the educational setting. I hope you enjoy, gain encouragement, and tolerate the zombie references to grasp the big picture and how it relates to us being better educators for the young people we serve.

-Introduction-

Chaos and mayhem surround you every day! You enter each room with extreme caution. First, peeking in quietly to assess your surroundings, then moving silently over the floor as an owl would glide through the night sky. You rejoice in those brief moments when you can sit and take a rest, even though you know your respite will soon be over.

Your mind and body have barely recovered from your last encounter, when in the distance you hear a faint noise. The sound resembles a hive of bees. It is a steady hum, which increases in volume as each second passes. At first, you think, *This is not happening! There is no way it could be starting again!* The hum gets louder and then you hear it...footsteps. These footsteps, though, do not sound like the steps of an organized group. As you hear various feet striking the floor you feel yourself starting to get anxious. You can see in your mind's eye a mob coming your way. You whisper to yourself, "Today is the day that they are going to eat me alive!" You think maybe if you wait quietly they will walk on by, not noticing you sitting in the dark corner.

For some odd reason, your mind vaguely recalls a book you read before "this" all started. That was a peaceful era when you had time to enjoy literature and stories that would take you to magical places. In that book, once considered fiction, you remember the author saying something about the ones now creeping toward you...they are attracted to noise. As that thought pours through your brain, your body reacts. You slow your breathing and stop all movements except for your eyes. Keeping your eyes still would be impossible because your mind tells you to look toward the door, you must observe "them" as they enter. You think to yourself, *I have done this before and I have survived. Today will be no different!* As you are unable to control the urge to glance at the room's opening, the noise level increases to its maximum volume.

Then it happens! At first, it is just one that enters. It is a girl, and she doesn't even look your way. Her jeans are torn and her oversized sweatshirt looks like it had not been washed in months. The shoes she has on are stained and frayed. The laces are untied and look dirty, and you can just imagine what they may smell like. Her lips are black, which matches her fingernails. She seems to be walking slow but with purpose, thankfully toward the back of the room.

You silently think to yourself, *Maybe staying quiet is working. The author of the book was correct! I can sit here silently and never be seen.* Your mind continues to race and you start questioning the plan of action that you have prepared for today. "Will it be enough?" you ask yourself quietly.

Then, three more appear. You see the beads of moisture on their heads and the smell hits your nostrils with nuclear force. This time, they are all boys. They are much louder but seem too interested in something else to notice you. Their clothes are worse than the girl's that came before them. They are more ragged, with holes throughout. The sleeves are torn off at the shoulder, allowing for the stench to flow freely from under their arms. All three have on boots that are covered with what you hope to be mud. They moan as they walk throughout your room, limping, and tripping over things, all the while still not looking in your direction. One has a bit of brown juice flowing from the corner of his mouth and a slight bulge in his lower lip. As he limps past the trash can he spits out something that looks like a wad of mud, it hits the bottom of the can with perfect precision. *Was that intentional?* You dismiss the thought as quickly as it came. You know there is no way "they" would even realize to do that...to spit. The group makes their way past you toward another corner of the room.

Your mind races, *I'm camouflaged! Or better yet-invisible.* Then a much larger one enters the room. He is dressed in what would have been nice attire at some point in the past. Now, the clothes just look wrinkled and worn. Dark circles are under his eyes and the tie that once looked like it had been tight against the top of his dress shirt is now sagging and hanging loosely, swaying back and forth as he slowly walks.

The image of the tie moving from side to side makes you think of the tire swing you used to play on as a little girl. What fun and excitement that swing brought you. For just a brief second you could feel the heat from the summer sun blanketing your face. The warm breeze would blow through your hair as you sailed through the sky. The last thing that crossed your mind as you let go of the swing and plunged into the cool water of the lake was that nothing would ever be more amazing than this. Such warm thoughts no longer have a place in this desolate world. A loud bell rings off in the distance and you dismiss the thought.

You focus your attention back on the lumbering figure that is making his way toward you. You have seen this man before. You always took pride in your ability to avoid him, but it looks like he finally has you cornered. Your mind races for a way to escape but this room only has one exit and it is blocked. To add to your anxiety several more boys and girls enter behind him. All have the same look of disgust on their face. Several actually get tripped up amongst each other and two fall to the ground knocking over several items from a nearby table in the process. In your mind, you scream, *The bell! The noise from the bell must have attracted them to my location!* You look toward the window and then at a nearby chair. A quick mental calculation allows you to determine that the window is about ten feet away. If the chair was thrown with enough force the glass should break easily. You realize you won't get out without a few injuries, but the reward is worth the risk. As you start to make your move the lumbering man moves closer toward you. Out of sheer fear you sit back down, frozen to your chair.

Then he speaks! You did not know they could still communicate! You had been told that he and others like him change. They no longer think as you do. They have forgotten what it was like to be "in your shoes" and the others in your alliance. All of their human elements have been removed. He looks directly at you and with a tired, gravelly voice groans, "Ms. Saunders, I hope you have enjoyed your planning period although I know it has not been long because we had to meet today to review some curriculum work. I see your students are now coming back from gym class. I thought since the state assessment is right around the corner this would be an excellent time to come do an "informal" site visit. I'll just be back here by the computers to see how things are going. By the way, if you see me on my phone, don't be offended. The district curriculum specialist is arranging a meeting to discuss the end-of-the-year data and I am awaiting his text. He said something about involving you as well, I'm sure you won't mind. I know you've got a lot to do right now, but I don't think it will take away from any class time. I will make sure we schedule it *after* school. Possibly this Friday?"

As Principal Lee makes his way toward the back corner, he stops by the trash can and looks down. A look of aggravation comes across his face when he addresses the class, "I see that someone has decided to spit their wad of chewing tobacco in the trash can...AGAIN! Let me remind you that you are all under the age of eighteen. If you are caught with ANY tobacco-related products you can be assured you will receive the maximum consequence the discipline handbook will allow!" As he walks off, the sleeveless boys in the back of the room look at each other and give a slight snicker. Before you rise from your chair to begin your lesson you think to yourself, *I'm just going to have to teach like it's the zombie apocalypse!*

Fiction or Nonfiction: A Depressing Reality

What you just read may have seemed like a work of fiction. Your mind may have been thinking this was a story coming from a comic book or sci-fi movie. Then you had a very sobering thought as you neared the end. *This is not some made up world coming from an imaginative genius...this is my own personal classroom!* Just like the teacher in the story, you too are dealing with: local and state assessments, loss of planning periods due to pointless meetings, data review conferences with district administrative teams, rowdy students who have a blatant disregard for the rules, mindless site visits and walkthroughs, and school level leadership that no longer realizes what it is like to be in the teacher's "shoes".

Challenging times in education can often feel like you are in a "zombie apocalypse". Oftentimes, I have heard teachers say something along the lines of, "Today is like a zombie movie, it is just about survival!" You may have had moments, days, weeks, or even years similar to this teacher. You may feel like you are truly in an apocalyptic time and your main focus is survival!

Whether you are walking into your first or hundredth classroom, knowing that you are solely responsible for the students that sit before you can be quite intimidating. Among the many thoughts that run through your mind is the idea that you are in no way prepared to be the main educator of this student body! Although, most teachers *feel* prepared prior to that moment, some aren't. I know you have spent countless hours and dollars acquiring the knowledge and skills necessary to make you not only an effective educator, but the best teacher you can be. All of that training and money has been well spent, let me assure you, it has given you the foundation necessary to be an effective and great educator.

I realize I just told you some teachers aren't prepared, but as you read on you will see how the knowledge and skills you have acquired in college, or even the most recent professional learning session will be paired with some realistic advice about how to become the teacher you have set out to be. You will then not only survive those difficult times-you will thrive!

There are a few things that cannot be taught in a university classroom, online, or even from professional learning seminars. There are many pieces to the puzzle of education that will create not only an effective school year, but a career that will be long-lasting and life-changing! So right about now, you are probably wondering about the magic pieces of that great puzzle, while at the same time wondering why no one shared all this information with you in college, or at the most recent professional learning development session.

In order to make it through an educational zombie apocalypse, you are going to have to prepare. Hopefully, it does not matter if you are in your first or twentieth year, you will gain a new or at least revived perspective into the classroom, and acquire some "weapons" and concepts to successfully make it through your educational career. These weapons and concepts will help you prepare for the difficult situations you are going to encounter along the way.

Although the great theories and many research-based practices are necessary, they will not pull you through the sometimes difficult, but always rewarding field of education. Everyone is not cut out for teaching. You must be passionate, resilient, and dedicated to the students.

You must be relentless in your quest for strategies that will improve your talents and your student's learning. In addition, you will want to build relationships with your colleagues, students, parents, and the community to help aid in the battle.

Remember, things will not always be clear, come easy, or seem logical, but using basic survival skills will keep you focused on the big picture and prevent you from getting hung up in the details! If you think you have what it takes, or you are in doubt whether or not you will make it through, keep reading!

A zombie takeover is a very serious matter and if you don't act fast, you will fall victim to the "biter" backlash! Apply the following chapters together as a whole and you will be fending off all types of problems that arise in what I call an educational zombie apocalypse! So, what is a teacher to do when faced with an educational zombie apocalypse? Simple! ***Teach like it's the zombie apocalypse!***

-Form Alliances-

As you walk into the room you immediately take a seat. The rest of your "team" is already positioned in the typical "U" formation. This design allows for optimal discussion between all members of the alliance. By some unspoken agreement you each just look at each other and give a slight nod of the head. A great peace and comfort flows through your body as you sit down. You feel safe and secure with this group. You have relied on each other for many years now, and today will be no different. Today you have been told by your commanding officer that you will review the "results" of the battle that occurred a few months back in the month of May. You have had similar discussions in the past, they always seem to come in the early autumn right after you have returned to "service" from your much-needed break. Your mind reflects on that May battle and you can see all the various forms of "zombies" that made themselves present during that five-day war. This meeting is to discuss the next steps of action based upon the war's outcome. As you begin to speculate about what will be discussed you hear a familiar noise. It is the sound of well-polished dress shoes tapping the tile floor as they make their way to the conference room. Your eyes shift toward the room's entrance, and then you see a tall lady walk in. She is dressed in all black with her hair pulled tight against her brow. With a stern look on her face she says, "Good afternoon! I appreciate you each taking time today to stay after school and meet with your grade level team. We will be discussing the results of last school year's standardized test that was conducted in May. We are being asked, by the state, to form a 30-60-90 day action plan based upon this information. Shall we begin?"

Form an alliance. It sounds logical and easy enough, right? Choosing your alliance wisely is a critical component of surviving and thriving in education. This is one time when quality and quantity go hand in hand. You need multiple alliances with quality people who will help you endure and overcome hardships. Fresh out of the university, you may have an alliance of first-year teachers who are also suffering from the gauntlet of first-year problems, another alliance of veteran teachers whom you look to for advice, some administrators or former professors who offer guidance and support, and even a social media presence to observe and participate in educational related discussions.

So, how does a teacher seek out an alliance that will help them thrive instead of perish? There is a multitude of factors that go into this alliance selection, so pay attention! Your passion, drive, reputation, longevity, and ultimately your survival depends on it!

Safety in Numbers

Of course there is a level of safety associated with numbers, but there is also a flip side to this concept. Quantity can be a good thing but it has to go hand in hand with quality. More than likely you have heard during your college coursework or district professional developments to beware of those who may seek you out when you join an organization for the first time, or possibly when you are placed in a new grade level with a new team of teachers. Why? Because often times those who seek you out first are the "Negative Nellies" and they will make it a point to recruit you early on.

This is a very difficult situation because not every staff member that approaches you first has a negative spirit. Actually, there will be some very genuine people that are the first to say hello and give you a pat on the back. The problem is being able to tell the difference at your first meeting. I wish it were simple. Unfortunately, it can be very difficult to distinguish between the two types of people.

Before you can truly form or join an alliance that will help you survive and thrive, you must become knowledgeable about those around you, their motives, current situations, their end goals, and of course you must also be aware of your own. So, the numbers thing can hurt you just as much as it can help, if you don't keep the word "quality" in the forefront of your mind. Don't just link up with anyone and take on their opinions and behaviors, but be positive and kind to all. You will figure things out as you go, and you do not need to have everything figured out within a specific time frame. Take your time, be thoughtful, and stay focused.

I also believe this is a key time to note the last thing education needs is another "Negative Nellie," so don't become one! I have spoken with several first-year teachers who seem to hate their job. I think to myself how miserable that person must be. They have invested a lot of time, money, and energy into something they openly say they don't enjoy. I am trying to help you avoid the downfall of being sucked into a "biter", "walker", or "undead mob". Take a moment to ground yourself in your purpose and motivation. I don't believe anyone goes into education selfishly, but rather because education is a profession where you receive rewards beyond monetary gain!

Unfortunately, many get "bit" early on and "turn". They never recover to realize their initial vision of being a positive and uplifting force within the field. Instead, they start to limp through the day, not really caring if additional bites are being taken out of them, because they too have joined in on the biting. They seek out others to gnash on, so they can cause their victims to "turn" and join the zombie mob. With that being said, you have to really hold fast to the reasons you became a teacher.

As you form alliances, keep your eye on the prize. Think about those "aha" moments, those special times when a student finally understands a concept they have been struggling with. We have all had those at some point. You are working with a struggling student and it finally clicks. You see this student and the excitement that comes from them being able to understand, and from that point forward they are able to soar with their new-found ability. They expand their wings to fly to higher places in their learning. As you battle the zombie hordes you begin to see these "aha" moments more often, and they will be your driving force. Know who you are and what your purpose is. You want your dream and the realization of that dream to survive the tough times, to avoid the "Negative Nellies," the uncertainty, the inexperience, and the exhausting daily grind.

While you are figuring things out and getting to know those around you, just stay positive, share your passion, and keep your focus on the students and their success! Do not, I repeat DO NOT get sucked into criticizing or judging other teachers, administrators, or schools. You also need to keep in mind that you are not building an alliance of people to just be social, drink coffee, and eat a doughnut with. You are building an elite professional educational task force that will help you withstand and overcome the many obstacles you are going to face. These challenges can be overwhelming at times, so it is essential to maintain a positive attitude, and surround yourself with people who will uplift and encourage you.

An important factor in having various alliances is knowing which alliance to find refuge with during various circumstances. If you are struggling in relation to content, you would be well-served to form a content related alliance within your building, district, or even a social media platform. If you are struggling with student behavior, you may be best advised by a group of veteran teachers or well-established administrators. If you are having difficulty adjusting to being a new teacher, a teacher in a new building, or an experienced teacher facing burnout, you may find comfort by talking with other teachers who are experiencing the same dilemma. You are surrounded by many experts in your building, seek them out!

During these times, you may feel like you are lost in the woods. You may very well hear the sounds of the undead all around you, seeking you out. They will not be satisfied until you too are wandering aimlessly with limited purpose. It will be in those times your alliances will be a critical component to help protect you, and assist in your return to "civilization" to that "gated community" of safety and comfort.

The Dangers of "False Security"

When a person puts faith and trust in something that is false they are only lying to themselves. The sad thing is many people would rather believe a lie than the truth in most cases. As you travel through a world of woes and troubles that is polluted with "zombies", you need to have confidence you are protected. Having a false sense of security is not only irresponsible, it is also extremely dangerous.

A fellow colleague very dear to me shared the following experience:

"I vividly recall graduating college ready to conquer the world and solve all of the problems in whatever classroom I would be fortunate enough to be employed. I wasn't at all arrogant, or at least that wasn't my intention. I, like many other college students and future teachers, worked very hard, volunteered for several years at my local elementary school, went to every professional development I could, attended special guest speaker events, read educational books, and worked very hard to excel in every endeavor. With all of that being said, my professors encouraged me, the mentor teachers I volunteered with bragged on me, administrators frequently praised my work ethic and dedication, especially since I was not getting paid. Although the support and encouragement were sincere and earned, I believe it gave me a false sense of security, which is extremely dangerous.

Oftentimes, people become too confident in themselves or their abilities. When this happens, it tends to lead down a bad path. People start to think that maybe they can survive any situation on their own. They start taking uncalculated risks and placing themselves and others in harm's way. In reality, I didn't know what was needed the day I entered my classroom and began my first full day of teaching. The number of hours I had logged, books I had read, speakers I had heard, or teachers I had talked to, in no way prepared me for what I faced that early August morning. The realization didn't take long to set in that not only was I unprepared, I may not even survive the first day! Things got "real", quick! The alliance "thing"- it was really important that afternoon. I needed some encouragement and reassurance that I could thrive and I hadn't already ruined my first year or the students' education."

You Don't Have to Be the Toughest or Smartest Person in the Group

I once heard someone say, a person should always have other people around them that are more intelligent than they are. At first, I didn't quite understand what this person was saying. To be frank, it didn't sound like a very intellectual statement at all. As I reflected on the comment, I began to realize the deeper meaning behind what was being said. They wanted me to surround myself with quality people who would support and lift me up in times of trouble. That may mean that they are more educated about particular topics, but it can also mean they simply have a different skill set.

In a true survival situation, you want to be around people who are smart, decisive, respectful, multi-talented, and have a physical and mental toughness. During those tough times in education, the moments in which you feel that you just can't take another minute, let alone day or year, you will find comfort in knowing you have a support system around you. You also need to realize those who stand beside you have, are, or will be experiencing the exact same troubles you are having.

If for some strange reason those around you are not currently fighting the same battles, there is a real good chance that they will in the future. There is an even better chance they just recently have come through a similar situation in the not so distant past. Troubles come to all people in all professions. Just remember you are not alone, and as long as you have a strong alliance you will be able to survive and thrive amidst the worst of times!

One of the best resources any educator can have is another educator. It truly takes all kinds of people to create an environment that will foster the learning, growth, and development of the diverse student body found in classrooms across our country. We all can't be great at everything, and teaching shouldn't be a one or two person job. What most successful people have in common is that they find others who compensate areas in which they lack. It's all about balance. You can't go into war with just one area of the battle plan thought out and ready, you need to have all areas covered. Various perspectives aren't a luxury in our chosen field, they are a must. Always be willing to ask for help! You don't have to know everything to survive, you simply have to surround yourself with others that can fill your gaps, and you will, in turn, fill theirs.

This, of course, isn't a new concept, but in the really tough times, the days where you think you are going to be eaten alive, it is easy to forget your alliances. As life happens and school days are logged, it is easy to forget that we are all on the same team and we need to utilize our players and plays. Unfortunately, some forget this concept, and when that happens things seem to turn into a competition. Don't get me wrong, I myself am quite competitive, but there is such a thing as healthy competition, and there is the type of competition that will be detrimental to the school environment, student achievement, and to relationships.

Healthy competition is the competition that will motivate and encourage a student, teacher, group, or school to work hard to do their best. On the other hand, destructive competition is where people are trying to outdo their neighbor, keeping strategies or resources to themselves in hopes of having a better outcome, and degrading others to make themselves look better. There is no place for this type of competition in the field of education.

Remember earlier when we discussed maintaining focus and choosing and building alliances? Don't think you always have to be the best, brightest, most outspoken, or front and center to make a difference. You are going to have to wear many different hats, or rather biohazard masks throughout your career, and you are going to have to find others to join your alliance that balance you! Keep in mind we all came into the field because we wanted to make a difference in the lives of students. Keep that focus no matter what. You are part of a team, and everyone needs to focus on doing their part to make the students, school, and team successful.

As you travel through what can sometimes be a bleak world with your alliance, be cautious about who and what lies behind every door. Take hope that you are not alone. Even though the fear of the undead and a host of other enemies lurk to destroy you and what you are trying to create...take hope that you are not alone. When you don't think you can go another step without being overtaken with a multitude of bites and tears...take hope that you are not alone! Fear is an extremely powerful motivator. Fear will get you up and moving toward a goal, but you have no need to fear. There is a much stronger motivating factor, that factor is hope. Hope is stronger than fear because hope is blanketed in love. Take hope in your alliance, show love and respect and you will in return receive it. By doing this, you will be well on a path to overcoming any and all educational zombies!

Survival Summary:

- ☣ Know the expertise of people as you form your alliance.
- ☣ Stay positive!
- ☣ Know your own weaknesses.
- ☣ Work toward a common goal.
- ☣ Hope is stronger than fear.

Dead Discussion:

1. Who do you see as your "alliance"?
2. In what ways are they assisting you? In what ways are you assisting them?

-Have a Cache of Weapons-

A small smile stretches across your face as you think about the array of arsenal you plan on using today. You know from experience that every day, every battle is different. Those who are infected are hard to defeat. The weapons you have chosen for this upcoming fight have not only been "designed" and chosen to defeat the "zombie" hordes, but will also be used to protect those who have not been bitten yet. You realize that in the past you have had some weapons fail you in battle, or simply not work. You have had other times where you have used up all your weapons well before the battle was over...that mistake will not happen today! You glance at your watch and see it won't be long now before "they" come to you. You will be outnumbered by twenty-four to one, but you have no fear. You quickly do a mental check of all the weapons that will be utilized today one final time. You say the following silently in your mind, "High quality lesson plan, engagement activities, prize jar is filled, wi-fi is working, electronic devices are fully charged, pencils are sharpened, dry erases markers are new and fresh, chart paper is hung, my coffee mug is filled, and I have a candy bar hidden in my top desk drawer! LET'S DO THIS!"

Defending yourself in a dangerous situation is critical. The number one rule to remember when faced with a crisis is to remain calm and protect yourself. The reason behind this is simple. How can you protect or benefit others, if you fall in battle? Whether you have been outrunning a deadly mob of mindless "half" humans who want nothing more than to sink their ugly teeth deep into your flesh, or you are fending off a group of young second graders who have sneezed on you more times then you could possibly imagine, you will need some tools. You will need "weapons"! When fighting, you will need to utilize an array of weaponry. The Bible even talks about spiritual warfare and the equipment that is needed to perform well in spiritual battles. This battle is no different. You need to utilize every weapon you have.

Unfortunately, the weapons on this battlefield are constantly changing, going from effective to ineffective, and what works in one circumstance, may not work in another. I once heard a teacher makes thousands of second by second decisions. A teacher is simultaneously assessing the conditions of an entire group, individuals, the environment, tools and resources that are needed, creating an environment for learning, organizational methods, addressing pop up battles (behaviors), and utilizing the many weapons in their arsenal, all the while, remaining on the battlefield.

Weapons come in all shapes, sizes, and forms. This weaponry can range from technology to classroom design to understanding the minds of those around you. The battle plans of a well-armed teacher aren't always something that can be verbalized or captured in a nice lesson plan; rather these plans include the ability to flip and turn on a dime, all the while maintaining focus and control of everyone on the battlefield!

It does not matter if you are new to teaching or have taught for a decade; I am sure you have heard the phrase, "This is just another tool in your toolbox." Those tools are important but can be overwhelming. Let's examine some of these tools I refer to as "weapons" that benefit teachers.

Consistent Management of Behavior

When dealing with a plague that is turning humans into nothing more than mindless flesh eaters you need to have a plan to survive and stick to the plan. Having a consistent classroom management plan in conjunction with a solid behavior system is no different. Like a zombie mob, negative behaviors can overcome even the most energetic teacher in a very short amount of time.

My father always uses the phrase, "A lack of consistency destroys." The only time this *may not* be true is if a person is either consistently inconsistent or consistently bad. Either way, being consistent in your inconsistencies or consistently doing a bad job are exceptions to the "lack of consistency destroys" rule. You see, even a zombie can be consistent. The way it moans. The way it creeps toward you with the same distinctive limp again and again. The zombie has bad intentions and it serves no good purpose. Therefore, a zombie's consistency is leading to terrible results.

When you are firm and consistent in your management of behavior, almost everything else will take care of itself. Several years ago, when I was a substitute teacher, I established behavior expectations from the first day. I wanted the students to know that I wanted to be respected and would be respectful to them. There are numerous classroom management systems that have been discussed by researchers and many I have personally tried. The key is to find a good system that works for you and stick with it. Address negative behaviors quickly and effectively.

For teachers who may be seeking a future in administration, understand that it is vital for you to ensure consistency across the entire school. That does not mean all teachers have to adopt a clip up or clip down behavior system. Absolutely do not make your sixth graders move their turtle from green to yellow like the kindergartners when they misbehave. It just simply means expectations need to be established and followed schoolwide.

Keep in mind the enemies you face in these very difficult times are not always educational zombies. Just like in a real zombie apocalypse, you will come across a whole host of enemies such as exposure to the elements, starvation, and potentially other humans who are taking advantage of a crisis situation for their own benefit. As you will read in the "Avoid Enemies" chapter of this book, those who are trying to harm you will come in all forms. Being consistent in how you handle behaviors and your own emotions, for both students and adults, will show how strong of an individual you are.

I think it is critical to share one key element that often goes unnoticed by many when the discussion of behavior and classroom management occurs. That key element is forming relationships. Being consistent, having a good system in place, and being prepared are all very critical pieces of this crazy puzzle. But relationships are what helps bind that puzzle together.

Even as I write this, my son and daughter are upstairs in their bedroom collecting puzzles for us to piece together. I enjoy puzzles. My family enjoys puzzles. Do you know what we like to do when we complete a puzzle? We like to get clear puzzle glue and coat that puzzle time and time again so all the pieces when displayed will hold together tight.

That is what relationships are. They are the glue that holds those other pieces of the puzzle together. Just like a puzzle, your behavior system, being prepared, and staying consistent will hold together nicely when laid on a flat undisturbed surface. What will happen when you go to move your puzzle, maybe put a bit of stress on the puzzle, ask a bit more from the puzzle then what it was designed for? Parts of the puzzle will break off in transit.

The same goes for your behavior management system. If there are no relationships that have been developed to glue the pieces together, you can expect some problems when trials and troubles come. Do not fear! You will overcome those hardships if you keep relationships in the forefront of your mind!

Positive and Negative Consequences

The word consequence is often associated with a negative connotation. Consequences are just a result of an action, and therefore can be both positive and negative. For example, a consequence of going to work is getting paid, a positive. A consequence of telling your principal to go take a hike, and he has no clue what you are going through may get you fired, a negative (although it probably felt awesome!)

Having an established set of positive and negative consequences ties directly to your need for a consistent management system for classroom behavior. This can be a tricky area for many. As a teacher, you need to make sure your principal or administrator is on board with your rewards (positive consequences) and punishments (negative consequences).

I once learned from a teacher of a terrible experience they had. The teacher had given a classroom assignment, clearly explained their expectations for what needed to be accomplished, and described the reward that was going to be given to those who performed well. In addition to setting clear expectations, they also reviewed what would occur if the assignment were not completed and the expectations were not met.

Seems pretty straightforward, right? Wrong! There was one student who did not meet the expectations because they refused to do the assignment altogether! As a result that student received a poor grade and did not get to participate in the reward with the rest of the class.

Days later the teacher was called into the principal's office and was forced to explain her reasoning for the consequence. The principal (in front of the parent) told the teacher that he disagreed with her actions. The teacher eventually had to give the discussed reward to the student, even though the student had not fulfilled the criteria that had been set forth in the assignment. I was told the relationship at that point between the principal and teacher had started to diminish. The teacher felt she was unsupported by her administrator.

Going forward, she was determined to always review with the principal, the positive and negative consequences prior to assignments or activities to ensure full support, just in case a similar situation were to arise. In doing this, she ensured full transparency and should be fully supported in her future decisions.

Rewards can come in all shapes and sizes. It can range from a candy jar treat to extra recess. One thing I always did was magic tricks. Yes, magic tricks. I would tell my students if they performed and behaved well, I would reward them with some sleight of hand. This worked for me more than anything else I could have done or purchased for that matter. I am not telling you to be the next Houdini or David Copperfield; but rather, rewards can be something that is easy, inexpensive, and meaningful to both your students and to you.

The final thing to consider when you are thinking about positive and negative consequences is that they must be directly tied to what motivates individual students. If sending a student home for the rest of the day is exactly what that student wants, then that student will continue the negative behavior because you have reinforced it. If you say you are going to have an ice cream party for all the students who got an "A" on a test, but the entire class is lactose intolerant, then the motivation to do well and receive the reward will more than likely be nonexistent. The point is simple, if the negative or positive consequence does not change the behavior, then change what you are doing.

Technology

Technology can either be a friend or foe; it depends on how well you utilize and manage it. There are many aspects of technology to be considered. When the subject of technology is introduced, we immediately start to discuss all of the ways students are, or could be using technology to increase their learning. Unfortunately, many don't look at how teachers, administrators, and parents are utilizing the technology, or managing student use of the technology.

First of all, in order to manage technology effectively, a teacher must be comfortable with the tools and resources that are available. In today's social media world, it is essential for teachers to use this virtual environment to reach out to parents and communities to gain support and provide information. There are new apps developed daily to help teachers and administrators achieve communication success. Remind 101, Class Messenger, and Class Dojo are a few that allow quick and easy daily communication. These tools allow teachers to quickly send home daily lessons, upcoming events, or even pictures. Never before has the ability to communicate with stakeholders been so effortless, but sadly it isn't always embraced as the valuable weapon that it is.

In addition to utilizing technology to communicate, teachers must have a strong knowledge base of the tools available and how they can be used to enhance, not detract, from the lesson objectives. It seems simple enough, but unfortunately, many teachers haven't been provided the education necessary to feel comfortable with technology integration. Many districts and schools are purchasing class sets of iPads, Chromebooks, or even laptops. Very few are offering the training necessary for teachers to understand how this technology should be effectively incorporated into daily activities. One thing you do not want to happen, is have your technology device serve as nothing more than an electronic worksheet.

If teachers aren't thoughtful with integration, the technology doesn't only become a distraction, it becomes a major time waster. If initial roll out of technology isn't well planned, it often results in frustrated teachers, unsuccessful integration, and behavior problems. Some teachers, if required to integrate and are improperly trained, will undoubtedly use the technology in the easiest, most obvious ways. These practices generally result in the students wasting valuable class time simply being consumers of pre-made programs with very little interaction. There are many applications that can be utilized to quickly and effectively present, assess, and engage students. Well thought out and quality professional development is a must when it comes to technology. What good is a weapon if you don't understand how and when to use it?

Another aspect that cannot be overlooked regarding technology, is what to do when the technology is misused. Inevitably, the technology is going to be misused by some teachers and several students. There must be a plan in place on how to monitor the use and effectiveness, as well as a protocol to follow when things aren't found to be at the level expected. Most teachers are going to address student misuse of technology on a daily basis so it is important to have a plan of action in place. There are several "watchdog" applications available to help monitor student usage a little easier. It is very important to understand the extreme value of this weapon, while at the same time understanding how it can also be the cause of a self-inflicted wound.

Engagement

We all have been there, sitting in a "professional learning" session actually wishing for the zombie apocalypse to occur because anything (even a flesh-eating mob creeping your way) would be more enjoyable than what is happening at that moment. Why? Is it because you are so knowledgeable about "all things educational" that you don't need the information? Maybe you showed up late and you are stuck with the only seat left, the seat right beside your principal. It could be the coffee and blueberry scone you ate moments earlier is beating the inside of your stomach and you need to get away fast, short of having the entire auditorium evacuate in a mass exodus as a result of a "toxic gas leak".

Although, all those things may add to the reason you are wishing that you was outrunning a crazed group of mindless beings, it is not the main reason. The main reason is the presenter is just so boring! You think to yourself the last time you have been this "engaged" was when you watched that late night documentary on the sea mollusk.

Your students feel the same way. You must find a way to lead your class through engaged instruction. I have found the number one way to do this is to become engaged yourself! You must be invested in what you are doing and be involved in the learning and teaching process that goes beyond a "pacing guide" or a "scope and sequence". If you are not passionate about what you are doing, the students will not be either!

Make sure you do not confuse engagement and entertainment. These two things can harmoniously be present, but you don't necessarily get them both each and every time. Students need to be cognitively engaged in the content, not simply entertained with a production. Students must get involved in the learning and the lesson. When students are listening, interacting with the content, and are doing something with the knowledge, engagement is truly taking place.

At one point in my career, I knew some things were going to have to change, and change fast, because it felt as though I was being eaten alive. So, what did I do? Well, I started to look at my "alliance" and listened to those around me. They had better insights into this "engagement piece" than I. What happened next was one of the greatest career experiences I had ever had. Instead of simply continuing to go through the motions and follow some cookie cutter guide to education, I became engaged. I sought out other professionals that had a proven track record of being successful. I asked myself and others around me some very hard questions, and I got some very hard answers in return. Those answers sparked the change that started to happen. Once the change was evident in me, others could see my level of engagement in myself had changed, and as a result, the level of engagement in those around me had also changed.

There are multiple ways to engage your students in learning and this is a fact that we all are aware of. There are many bestselling books, which sell thousands upon thousands of copies because they offer new or sometimes reworded ways to engage students in learning. Whether you are using a clicker system where students can present answers in real time, cutting out huge pieces of dry erase board that will cover entire desk or tables that allow students to write and erase answers with ease, utilizing the most advanced pieces of technology, or following proven discussion strategies with talk partners, you need to find multiple ways to engage students.

You also need to understand what works one day, may not work on another. What works with one group of kids, may not work with the other group. The key is to arm yourself with a few different engagement techniques and utilize them to the best of your ability. As you have time to research and test other strategies, add them to your arsenal. Within a very short time, you are going to have a bow in your cache of weapons that can shoot multiple sources of arrows, and I can assure you those arrows will find their mark and make a positive difference not only in your teaching but in the lives of young people.

Understanding the Mind

Understanding the mind will be touched upon more in the chapter titled, "Attack the Brain" but it does not need to be neglected as a weapon. This may be one of the most powerful weapons you can have at your disposal. I think it has been made very clear that multiple enemies surround us in this educational apocalypse. We have the flesh biters who are the obvious enemy, but there are other forces that are more subtle; such as that one parent who takes every opportunity they can to degrade you on social media. The weapon of understanding the mind will work for all forms of enemies. When you understand who and what you are dealing with, what motivates or discourages them, you are much more equipped at that point to formulate a plan of attack.

Survival Summary:

- ☣ Establish relationships first.
- ☣ Be consistent.
- ☣ Consequences are negative/positive and must be tied directly to a motivating factor.
- ☣ Set clear expectations.
- ☣ Involve all stakeholders in the discipline process.
- ☣ Utilize technology effectively.
- ☣ Create strong engagement lessons.
- ☣ Understand the enemy.

Dead Discussion:

1. What "weapons" do you prefer to use in your teaching?
2. Do you think your "weapons" are effective and making a positive change in the lives of young people? How do you know?
3. Are your weapon choices supported with data or do you simply use them because they are familiar/easy?

-Rest Up-

As you look around you see the destruction of the most recent battle. You still are confused as to what happened. Just moments ago, you were fending off hordes of zombies. They were coming at you from all angles. Then, all of the sudden a loud bell rang, and they all stopped attacking. It was like they were internally programed somehow to flee to a set location upon hearing the sound. As you examine the damage that has been caused you see a chair turned upside down on the floor. You reach for it slowly, your body aches from not only this battle but the hundreds of other battles you have been forced to fight the last several weeks. You sit the chair upright and then allow your body to collapse into it. You knew today would be the final fight for a while, but you can't help but reflect upon all the "bites", "scratches", and days of not having enough time to even eat a lunch over the past few months. Your commander said you would be dispatched for recovery for about the next eight weeks. In your heart you know it will not be that long. You have been given similar promises in the past and the furlough you are given always seems much shorter than the original projection. As you wipe the unhappy thoughts from your mind you can't help but think to yourself, "I am so happy that summer break starts tomorrow!"

While conducting some of my advanced coursework for higher degrees I read a few books dealing with the importance of rest. The more modern-day term is self-care. One of the greatest dangers facing the future of educators is not a world filled with animated corpses trying to bite and "turn" the entire human race. The main danger is burnout!

In years past this would be a term set aside for those veteran teachers who have been in the trenches of education for years. Not anymore! Often times you are hearing the term spill out of the mouths of even non-tenured teachers who barely have less than a handful of years under their belt.

Burnout can be caused by many factors. When talking with others in the profession who have allowed this term to slip from their tongue it was easy to create a list of what is adding to early burnout. Many of the reasons dealt with constant changes in academic standards, discipline problems, unsupportive parents and stakeholders, unnecessary meetings during and after school hours, poor leadership and political issues that hinder and undermine teachers. When these issues are compounded, they lead to people simply "being tired!"

A good word to use here is balance. As educators, we all know that we are going to need to work and prepare beyond the school day at times. My suggestion would be to utilize your time effectively. Your moments of "rest" are really not peaceful if you have a whole list of things to complete for the next day or coming weeks. I would ask that you really evaluate your daily routines, find and eliminate time wasters, utilize the new-found time to accomplish the most important tasks, and then rest when the time comes.

Being exhausted is common for the highly engaged teacher. You are always going above and beyond to make a difference. As you strive for student achievement you sacrifice your own body and mind with late nights and early mornings. You have to realize the importance of rest. The educational undead will never stop! They will slowly and steadily limp toward you with teeth clenched. It does you no good when you are in a safe place to still continue to expend energy on something that 1) cannot reach you and 2) you cannot control. So, what you need to do in those times of safety is very simple, REST!

Content Planning Times

Hopefully, you are employed at a school where you are able to receive a "planning" time. If so, in the best-case scenario, you are able to receive that planning time on a daily basis and it lasts somewhere between forty minutes to an hour. Planning is an essential part of the teaching and learning process. In order to present engaging, successful lessons, you must have time to prepare your battle plan and gather your weaponry.

Unfortunately, those who do receive a planning time "on paper" or "it is built in the schedule" often don't see their planning period because of parent conferences, special education meetings, professional learning community sessions, being asked to cover for absent teachers or even choosing to offer additional tutoring to struggling students.

The advice offered here is you need to take advantage of your planning periods. This is a time that is set aside, if at all possible, for you to rest, reflect, organize your thoughts, and prepare for battle. It is the only time, other than the brief moment you get to eat lunch (where you are 100% convinced time literally speeds up), to be alone with your thoughts and step away from some educational zombies.

People in education love children, or at least they should, but that does not mean they don't need a break. Several teachers have shared over the years that their planning period is one of the things that has allowed them to successfully make it through the day. If it is regarded as such a priceless time to so many, you cannot afford to let it slip past.

Sadly, I admit, my thoughts as an administrator have not always been this way in regards to a teacher's planning period. When I first started out as a principal, I was too preoccupied with things I thought were important but in reality, they were not. It was not until I really started interacting with my staff and seeking their input that I realized these short times during the day were essential in overcoming educational zombies.

I can proudly say today, since I have come to the "planning revelation", I personally make every effort to ensure all teachers get their planning period as much as possible. Sure, there are times we have to hold meetings with parents to update an IEP for a special education student or we need to get together for a brief PLC. Those meetings are natural and cannot be avoided. Often times those meetings, through a true collaboration process can even be energizing! What can be avoided is all the "extra" meetings that can be removed because the same information can be presented in a five-minute email.

The school I am blessed to lead has been extremely successful. I contribute a large portion of the success to my teachers not feeling burdened with foolish meetings. My staff know, no matter what, their planning time will be protected! Even if that means I (as the principal) am teaching art, leading computer lab, or going back to my P.E. teaching days and showing kids how to juggle! Planning times are precious and need to be preserved and protected at all cost!

If you feel like your planning time is being wasted on things that "really don't matter", I would encourage you to speak to your administrator. Some of the greatest changes that have been brought about at my school, have been based upon teacher led suggestions. If you feel unsure about how to approach your administrator, seek out an alliance member to guide you. Keep in mind, timing is everything when offering suggestions. Look for a time when at least a few "zombies" and educational related problems are out of the way, and use that as an opportunity to bring up your ideas.

Evenings

Long days and short nights will lead to extreme exhaustion. One of the biggest problems I face is not being able to turn off my mind once I leave work. Even though my body is far away from the school building, my thoughts are continually on either what I have not accomplished or what I need to accomplish. This is very dangerous territory because this does not only affect your own mind and mental health, but it starts impacting those around you that you love.

A very dear friend and a wise man once discussed in a church service the topic of underwater currents. He explained that even though things look calm on the surface, there is always a current moving under the water. We all need to realize no matter how many items we check off our list, there is always going to be more to do. There is always an undercurrent that will never cease! With that said, you need to dedicate your evenings to your family and friends, leave work at work! What I have learned by doing this, is my mind is much clearer, and I am more productive when it is actually time to "suit up" the next morning.

Those few hours in the evenings, as short as they may be, can keep you energized to face a new wave of educational zombies or any other adversary each day head-on. In addition to making you more productive at work, this time will also be beneficial to your family, personal well-being, and relationships.

Weekends

I can vividly recall a school year where the district I work in hired a new superintendent. The lady did an amazing job and I remember her saying something very personal to me. She shared with me a brief story of some career and life experiences she had and when she finished, she told me what she felt was my greatest fault. Her statement was simple. She told me my biggest problem was that I go too hard too fast, and if I was not careful, I was going to burnout at a young age. I was thirty years old at the time. In addition to the burnout, she said if I was not mindful, I would harm those around me that I loved the most.

For that reason alone, I try to dedicate each weekend to my family. By doing this we all have something to look forward to throughout the work week. I will often send a text on my lunch break to my wife and give ideas for our weekend. We don't do anything extravagant but we do spend time together. It does not matter if we grab a hotdog and milkshake and eat in the park, go to the local flea market, antique shops or add to my personal library by visiting the Goodwill bookstore, we take time to be together and save all the zombie slaying for Monday.

Vacation Breaks

They are called "breaks" for a reason. You need to take a break. If we were all to be honest, a variety of vacation time would probably be in everyone's top five personal reasons for going into the field of education in the first place. For those who are reading this and whose children attend school within the same district you are employed, you understand the perks. If there is a snow day and school is canceled, there is a good chance you are home building a snowman with your child. In addition to the beloved snow day, you are always guaranteed to be home for various holidays with your family. Even if your child does not attend the same district in which you are employed, the chances of being off at the same times are fairly good. Then there is the pinnacle of all breaks, the grand prize, summer break!

If in the summer all you are doing is stewing over the past year or planning for the upcoming year, what is the point of the break? Remember earlier when we discussed the part about battles? You are either currently in a battle of some sort, you have just come out of a battle, or there is a battle awaiting you in the future. With that being said you have got to take time to rest. The terrible and stressful year you just had is over! There is nothing more you can do about that year. It is in the past and no matter how much you stew on, regret, worry, or replay it in your mind, you cannot "will" it to be any different than what it was. It was an "apocalyptic year" and now it is over! In addition, you cannot do a thing about what may happen in the future. Often times we worry and stress more about things that never come to pass simply because we will not let our mind rest.

I know as much as anyone that tough times exist and will always exist. That is why it is so critical to take all the time you can to rest up. In doing so you are going to be much more equipped to deal with the next wave of educational zombies that are coming your way. Also, don't forget what was mentioned about being in a crisis situation. If you do not take care of yourself you will be useless to all others around you. In today's world of increased pressure for "academic results" you need to be as prepared as possible, and one of the greatest ways to prepare is to get rested up.

Survival Summary:

- If you are in a safe place-REST!
- Value your planning period.
- At times of "breaks"-take a break!
- Control what you can control.
- Know there is always going to be an "undercurrent".
- Don't create unneeded stress and worry with "imagined problems".

Dead Discussion:

1. What changes could you make within your work routine to make your times of rest more effective?
2. When do you have periods of rest, what prevents you from enjoying those times?
3. Working beyond the school day is often times a must to feel well prepared, how can you balance those extra times of work with rest?
4. Make a list of the things that "you CAN NOT control" and remove those things from your worries.

-Seek Shelter-

Your pace quickens as you look at your watch. You realize time is running out before your battle begins to rage again. Although, this time the battle will be a bit different. Your local intelligence team has informed you that this enemy has been seeking you out for some time. They have taken multiple "bites" out of you by attacking your character through various communication platforms that some refer to as "social media". You are convinced that if given the opportunity they will gladly, "have you for lunch". As you turn the corner you look for a place to seek some quick refuge, some shelter to get your thoughts together. You scan the vast variety of doors that align each side of the hallway. Then one stands out like a beacon of light. It has a symbol on the front that represent the human male form. You have used this location in times past because of its vast amount of privacy. As quickly as you open the door you close it, and immediately latch the lock, indicating to those on the outside that this location is now "occupied". There is only one place to sit, and you quickly take advantage for a short rest. Then you hear the most dreaded sound you could ever hear while sitting in this small room. A knock followed by a voice! "Mr. Brantley, I am sorry to interrupt you, but I just saw you step in the faculty bathroom, I wanted to let you know that your one o'clock meeting about the discipline issue you handled last week is here. Just a heads up, the parents seem pretty upset."

You can read any book, article, or magazine that deals with survival, as well as watch any documentary or reality TV show where people are asked to manage for three weeks in some uncharted wilderness, and you will always come across a common theme. Seek shelter!

Shelter secures us from the elements that are all around. In a true undead apocalyptic situation, people are often forced to leave their "home" and are left to the elements of nature. The faster they can find a safe place to protect themselves, the better off they are going to be.

Being in a school system is no different. We have already touched upon many of the things that would make a school year difficult. One of the most common things that make the lives of teachers so hard, is they are forced to leave their "comfort" zone.

Leaving your comfort zone could mean many things. Maybe you have been transferred to a different school, grade level, or more drastically you have left a school district or state, and are now in an entirely new area. You are possibly being asked to work with a colleague that you personally don't "collaborate" well with, or your district and state are forcing new requirements upon you that seem very far-fetched and pointless. Whatever the case may be, you are sensing educational zombies all around and now that you have officially left your nice comfortable "home" you have to find another place to seek refuge.

Classroom

When having these thoughts, the first obvious shelter that came to my mind would be your own classroom. In some cases it may even be the same physical classroom. But now because of the situation you have been placed in (i.e. moved to a new grade level) you may no longer feel as comfortable. Your old, comfortable room now seems unfamiliar or "new".

Remember, you are a very smart individual with a unique skill set. No matter what content or grade you are teaching, you still are *you!* You have abilities, skills, and are special. Even if you are in a new area establishing a new shelter you still have your "old" talents that have allowed you to survive in the past, so utilize those talents.

Your Alliance Will Help Protect You

Do you remember earlier when we talked about forming alliances, and we gave some examples of who those alliances could be? That is a great place to find some protective shelter. Those alliances are going to be able to help you in establishing a new safe place. Those who have "your back" will keep you safe! By ensuring your safety they are helping to secure their own as well.

Imagine this, a true zombie apocalypse has occurred and you have to leave your home and are seeking a new shelter, the sun is setting deep in the west and darkness is creeping in from the east. You and your alliance, which consist of hardened warriors are moving through the countryside seeking that much-needed place of refuge. As the light continues to dim you all come to the realization the thought of finding a secure shelter for the evening, like the light, is also fading. You all determine the best plan of action is to make camp for the night but you each have the fear that the undead will come upon you as you sleep.

What do you all do? The only logical thing you can do, you keep watch! You each agree to set up a rotation through the night, where at least one member of your trusted alliance will sacrifice much-needed sleep for a period of time, while the remaining alliance members rest. What allows this system to work? It works because all members of the group each sacrifice a little for the betterment of the entire alliance.

As you are facing a difficult time in your career or life for that matter, and you have no true fortress to hide in, you have to rely upon those you trust the most. Some of us are more fortunate than others to have an alliance that consists of many members. Even if your group of trusted colleagues is small, take hope in the fact that they are still powerful.

Just remember that you are also a part of that group. Sure, people will make sacrifices in their life and career to help you in difficult times, but don't forget that you too are a part of the "night watch rotation". This means you have to be willing to step up and make the same sacrifices for them. By doing this process you will learn that when all give a little, a lot can get accomplished. As a result, you have successfully survived another dark night and have kept the undead at bay.

Routines

Shelter can come in all forms. Evaluate what you are skilled at and what you can control, then use that to your advantage. A great "controllable" in your life should be your routines. Routines are a wonderful way for you to feel protected. One of my personal favorite routines is to be early wherever I go and to establish a comfort zone.

For example, if you were hosting a party who would be at your home for the party *before* you? Silly question, right? Of course, no one would be at your own home before the party started other than you and your family. That is what makes your home yours! You are already there! You have established a comfort zone for yourself. The point here is that people are coming to you. It is always easier when you have to be in a strange place, to get there before everyone else to become acquainted with the environment and settle your nerves.

This sets up the scenario that others (parents, students, administrators, fellow teachers, or community members) are coming in on your "party" like you are the host. Apply this to your new placement, school, or district. When there is a meeting, try to be early. If there is a meet the teacher night, be the first one there. At your district's professional development sessions don't be the one person sneaking in after the presenter is already talking. Never walk into a classroom where a fresh group of students are already sitting and waiting. Remember, even though the situation is not ideal, you still are seeking a level of protection through new shelter. When people come to you as opposed to you going to them, you will have an advantage that will make you feel stronger and more protected. In addition to all the other benefits when you are the first to arrive at a location you will know where two critical places are early on: the bathroom and the exit!

Survival Summary:

- ☣ When in a "new environment" remember you still have "old talents".
- ☣ Rely on your alliance members-they are relying on you.
- ☣ Have set routines!
- ☣ Arrive early and establish a safe area where others are coming to you (parent teacher conference, open house, classroom, professional learning sessions, and grade level meetings).

Dead Discussion:

1. When do you feel the "safest"?
2. What can you do to ensure the majority of your interactions are in your "safe zone" or "shelter"?
3. When you have no "shelter" near you, what is your plan of action in dealing with situations?

-Attack the Brain-

For many days now, sleep has escaped you. As you lie on your back looking straight up, all you can see is darkness, even though your eyes are wide open. You have received a critical piece of information that will make all the difference in your battles from this point forward. The message delivered was short and simple. It said, "Attack the brain!" This small bit of information came as no real surprise. You have been in many battles, but you never could figure out why you were not "getting through" to the enemy. Why you were not able to overcome the zombies! Tomorrow will be different! You have strategically planned to attack the minds of those who are trying to "eat you alive", by finding out what motivates them to do what they do. You finally close your eyes and drift off to sleep while thinking to yourself, "The second semester of this school year is going to go much smoother now that I understand the minds of my students!"

A true zombie aficionado knows the ONLY way to stop the undead is to attack the brain. The walking corpse could be missing limbs, have no eyes, or a spear through the heart, and it will keep coming at you until you address their only weakness. The only way to defeat it is to pierce that vital organ that rests between the ears.

Dealing with educational zombies is no different. Once you can penetrate the mind of those who are trying to tear your flesh apart, you are on the correct path to survival. Please don't forget, educational zombies come in all types. Some days it can be your students, and on other days it may be your co-workers, parents, or administrators. It is important to know how to deal with each one's mind.

Brain vs. Brain

Don't ever forget you are a smart person. There is a strong chance you were chosen among many other applicants for the job you have. If you are late in your career, there is an even better chance that many of you have college credit hours that extend well beyond a master's degree. There is no secret formula that can be presented here. You simply need to try to understand the minds of those around you to the very best of your ability. You will then quickly learn what you can do to make each day successful.

In my career, I have been amazed that there are people (some that hold high ranking positions in the field of education) that still miss this concept. They still do not understand how to penetrate the internal workings of the minds of others. They fail to place themselves in the shoes of those they are trying to lead. This concept is so critical. You must understand those who are trying to do you harm before you can have a clear and efficient plan of attack.

Think about this, a person does not wake up one morning and say, "Hey, I am going to become a flesh eater today!" No! Zombies are infected. They are a result of something beyond their control-a deadly virus. The educational zombies we face are no different in many regards. They are a result of their life's experiences. They have been bitten themselves and have turned! That is why we don't only need to defeat these zombies as they approach us, but we need to be working to find a cure for the infected.

Look for a Cure

The biggest fear that I have while writing this section, is that I will steer you away from the positive and overall encouraging nature of the book. If you are not careful while formulating a plan of attack, you may start seeing nothing but educational zombies all around you. If all you think about is the negative, then all you are going to see in life is the negative.

How does one defeat negativity? How can a teacher cure all the educational zombies they are facing? The best answer is with a good positive attitude! If educators want to combat poor infrastructure, unrealistic standards, ridiculous meetings, unsupportive leadership, disengaged coworkers, and numerous other school related undead enemies then you must stay encouraged! This is not an easy thing to do! Life on a very good day can still be difficult. Life riddled with problems and negativity is downright hard! Staying encouraged and positive allows you to formulate a plan of attack. It allows you to stay calm. You can gather information and then make calculated decisions based upon a thorough assessment of the various problems.

Our educational zombies need to be cured, but it will take time. My suggestion would be to start with the simplest zombie forms and try to cure them first. Understanding and attacking the minds of our educational zombies is a good first step in finding a cure!

Survival Summary:

- ☣ Understand the enemy's mind and attack it!
- ☣ Your brain is a powerful weapon.
- ☣ Remember- "zombies" started out as humans before they were infected.
- ☣ Don't waste energy on being negative.
- ☣ Search for a cure-be a positive influence!

Dead Discussion:

1. What could you change about your own actions to create a more positive culture?
2. What could you do to understand more about the mind of your enemy?

-Avoid Enemies-

The day is half over, and you feel like the morning has been successful. You take joy in the fact that you have had no battles against any of the "infected" thus far. As you make your way from the "mess hall", where you have just dropped off those you have been assigned to supervise to eat their mid-day meal. You make your way to a nearby room that is only for "authorized personnel". As your hand reaches toward the door handle, you notice something out of the corner of your eye. It is one of your fellow alliance members practically running down the hall waving her arms silently. Upon approaching you, she leans in toward your ear and whispers, "Don't go in there! I just saw three C.A.P.E. members walk in!" You pull back your hand as if the door handle was a viper getting ready to strike. You start to slowly walk away backwards, not taking your eye off the door in fear that they would walk out at any second. C.A.P.E is the code name you and your alliance have assigned to a small group of people that make up the minority of your organization. Although, they are not fully infected you fear they are very susceptible to being bit and then "turning" into those vicious beings. They are called the C.A.P.E. group because they are the ones that, "Complain About People and Everything else". They have an extremely negative outlook not only on the organization, but life in general. You then ask yourself a very important question, "Is going in the teacher's lounge to get a nice cold drink worth facing this negative group?"

Form alliances! Avoid enemies! Even the simplest of concepts require focus, time, and effort. Very early on we discussed that you should form alliances. In the same token, you should do something that seems extremely obvious. That is to avoid enemies! As mentioned, enemies can take on all forms and each one must be dealt with differently. Those who try to oppose you can come from within or from outside of your organization. Some enemies cannot be avoided no matter what, while others can. If you have not learned by now, I am a huge nerd (not to be confused with a geek).

For further clarification on the difference between nerd and geek, I would like to reference Baxter Stockman and April O'Neil's conversation early on in the 2016 Ninja Turtles Movie "Out of the Shadows". Geeks are described as being more on the lines of computer hackers and tech experts whereas nerds are more like the people who read comics and play video games, or in this case write an encouraging educational resource with zombie references throughout. Fortunately, while growing up as a nerd, I got very skilled at simply avoiding enemies.

To put this in perspective let's take a small trip into the fictional future about three years past a terrible governmental experiment that has just gone wrong. Now a third of the world's population is ravished by a terrible illness. This illness converts those who have died into walking flesh biters. You and your alliance have not eaten for days and the only food you can find is in nearby mall food court riddled with these undead beings who would love nothing more than to eat your face. This is an example of an enemy that simply cannot be avoided. You have to eat or you are not going to make it another day.

This scenario is very similar to the educational enemies that you have to deal with on a daily basis. You need to be mindful of those weapons we discussed that can help you deal with those enemies. Examples of these enemies could range from your problem students, grouchy co-workers, weak financial funding, over assessing, and silly supervisors. No matter who is trying to attack and bring you down, take a moment to evaluate the situation, select an appropriate educational "weapon", and attack the brain!

Now let's go back to the fictional future, to the mall where we were a few moments ago. You have defeated the enemy by attacking the brain with one of the weapons in your arsenal and are now ready to leave the mall. You look up and observe two exits. Exit A is blocked with an undead mob on the other side just waiting to have your group for their next meal while Exit B is clear and safe. What exit do you choose? Of course, you go out Exit B!

You need to practice that same decision making as you travel through an educational zombie apocalypse. If there are people, places or situations that can be avoided, then do just that, avoid them! I once read some advice about dealing with difficult people. The heart of the message was this, the best way to handle most situations is to walk away, or in other words, avoid it. Even the best fighters sometimes just need a break.

By avoiding educational zombies and other enemies, you will start to learn very quickly that your professional life will drastically improve. Guess what else will start to happen? You will have more energy to take on the enemies that cannot be avoided. This is due to the fact you have no longer wasted your time on educational zombies, other enemies, or situations that simply were able to be left alone.

Internal and External Enemies

At the beginning of this chapter a comparison was made about how enemies are similar to alliance members. Like those in your alliance, educational enemies can take on all shapes, sizes, and forms. When thinking of enemies, my mind naturally goes to internal and external, the two main types.

First, I think of enemies that come from outside of our organization. We will refer to these as external enemies. An example may be a student or parent that had a bad educational experience growing up. They often place all their disdain for learning right in your lap as the teacher. Outside enemies could also be those few community members that really want to pick apart your organization. They enjoy and look for opportunities to promote your mistakes on social media.

You may also encounter enemies from a state or federal level that are trying to destroy you and your profession. I will never forget the year our state was going through a massive retirement system reform. Many folks felt they were not valued and a promise that was made to them upon entering the education workforce was now about to be broken. This added to all the other educational zombies that were trying to take bites out of them. This made for a very difficult time for thousands of educators.

Outside enemies are hard to deal with, but there is one good thing about them. You usually know who they are! You can see the torn clothing, the gnashing teeth, and the long fingernails. You can smell the rotten flesh that sags from their bones. The outside enemies are those main educational zombies that slowly and steadily creep your way. They are dangerous and want to destroy you, but stand firm in the fact that you know who they are, and you know how to defend yourself.

Secondly, I think of enemies that are inside your organization. These internal enemies are often fewer in number than those who are coming from the outside. Don't let the small number fool you, they are just as dangerous! What makes them so dangerous? They are dangerous because they are often overlooked due to the fact they are harder to identify.

For those reading this and are somewhat involved with actual zombie culture, you will know that these are the enemies that are very much *living*. These are not always the undead zombies that can be spotted from a distance, rather these are the folks stealing extra food from the pantry in a time of extreme rations. These are the people that may say they have your back, when really the only reason they are "behind you" is because it is easier to trip someone from behind. The encouraging pat on the back you may receive, could be that person searching for a soft spot to stick a knife. These enemies are the silent killers. These enemies often are looking out for only one person, and that person certainly isn't you! Internal enemies could just as easily be the teacher two doors down from you or your very own instructional assistant!

The best way to deal with these enemies is first to recognize them and their motives. Often times it is the people in an organization that are experiencing a lack of fulfillment. As a result of their unmet professional needs, they want to destroy everyone else! People who are hurting, often times want to hurt other people. Deal with these enemies in a kind way but keep a safe distance. Be aware of what they are trying to do, then, as mentioned earlier, don't allow yourself to be a part of their negative culture.

The Living and the Living Dead

Now that you have been introduced to the main two types of enemies, I would like to take just a moment to expand on these enemies.

I will start first with the living dead or undead enemy. These are what we are calling the educational zombies. Remember they are easier to spot. As I've already stated, you can see, hear, and smell them way off in the distance. They don't even try to hide that they are coming for you. They are the obvious enemy. There is though, one interesting fact that all my actual zombie research has shown me. That fact is that zombies are attracted to the living...not the dead!

Why is this fact so important? It is important because it allows you to have a cloak of invincibility. Why is it that a zombie will limp right pass a human already dying of some incurable ailment? It is because, once again, zombies are attracted to the living!

True zombies are infected with a parasite that need a healthy host. They don't attack those who are very near death, because there is no need to. Remember, the terrible disease that is spreading through the world converts all who die into a zombie. The person who is going to die due to some other illness is going to turn into a zombie anyway in just a short amount of time.

Consider this, why would a group of completely healthy humans cover themselves with the entrails of a zombie they have defeated? What would allow them to then stroll through a walker mob seemingly unnoticed? It's because the undead does not bite those who are covered in zombie guts because they assume those covered are already zombies! What is the point of this brief history lesson in zombie victim selection?

The point goes back to hope! You can take hope in the fact there is a system of camouflage. What I am trying to say, is you can avoid the undead even when you really can't *physically* avoid them. There may be times you have to walk right past a slobbering mob of educational zombies and you do not have any weapons, resources, or energy to fight. In that case, know how to, for a brief moment, camouflage your fears and just sneak right past those who are trying to take you out.

As I have stated already, I love to read. I probably inherited the trait from my father who is also an avid lover of books. In addition to me being this massive sci-fi nerd, I consider myself somewhat of a cowboy. Now I imagine you are at this moment getting a really weird mental image of me. That's ok...I'm used to it. So, along with all of the zombie, hobbit, elven, dragon, and alchemist books, I also love reading westerns!

I will be the first to admit that what I am about to say is not an easy thing to actually do. This concept is inspired by a book I have read at least four times called Flint by Louis L'aMour.

Basically, the main character, James, was raised and trained by an older man named Flint. Flint taught James to never allow other people to know what "harmed him". Flint explained to James that when your enemies know what "gets under your skin" they will use that information against you in some way to further their own personal cause.

For this reason, you must always put on a brave face. Even when you are rattled or upset, try not to let it show. Because once people know your "kryptonite", they will use that to bring you aggravation and discomfort.

Don't get me wrong. I am not saying you need to be a fake. All I am suggesting is in a world where everyone wants to share their mind and feelings with all who will listen, be one of the few who stands apart. Have tact and be discreet. Keep the things that bother you the most between you and only your trusted alliance.

So, in a sense, both the living and the not so living enemies can be avoided by taking on a sense of camouflage. Whether you are trying to blend in and sneak past for a minute or you are simply putting on a tough exterior, you are making yourself invisible, allowing you to move on past both types of enemies!

Survival Summary:

- Avoid enemies when you can.
- Conserve your energy for the battles you know you will have to fight.
- External enemies are often easier to spot, and are in most cases what we refer to as an educational zombie.
- Internal enemies can take on both the educational zombie form but many are also "living enemies" that may be fewer in number but just as deadly!
- Find a way to camouflage your fears and what bothers you.
- Trust only those you feel the closest to.

Dead Discussion:

1. List your past, current, and possible future "enemies". (Problematic students, fellow teachers, administrators, state officials, parents, laws/regulations, academic standards, facilities, etc.) Are these internal or external enemies?
2. Are there particular times when these enemies are present?
3. How are you going to handle these "enemies"? (Don't forget that educational zombies are different than living enemies)

-Be Resourceful-

*You have simply come to accept the odd looks you
receive from others. You no longer care what they think.
As each year passes you have seen a common trend. You
have noticed the "defense budget" has been cut drastically,
although the battle against the "undead" still wages on.
Year after year you are assigned new recruits and it is your
responsibility to care for them, to "teach" them! The
problem is that each year it seems like the number of
infected that come along undetected into your organization
is greater. This makes no difference! Even with problems
arising all around you there will be no additional funding
assigned to your sector. That is why you have collected
and stored what others may refer to as "trash" or
"garbage". You can see the value of many things beyond
how they appear at the surface. You have learned that
these collected supplies will serve a greater good in the
coming months. As you stare at your three open filing
cabinets you say out loud to no one in particular, "All of
this tissue paper, rubber bands, toilet paper rolls, Popsicle
sticks, used food jars, empty coffee cans and buttons could
come in handy for a project this school year. I better hold
off on throwing any of it away."*

I saw a statement once that basically said if there
was an actual zombie apocalypse, the only people who
would be able to survive would be teachers. Due to the fact
they know how to get through life with the least amount of
resources. Most of us, if we are being truthful, can say
across the board in our life we have our needs met and in
most cases many of our wants.

When it comes to your "school world" on the other
hand, there is a good chance you may feel you are lacking
critical provisions that will aid in your educational

survival. In those particular circumstances, you will need to be resourceful.

Being resourceful means you are able to react and adapt to a variety of situations by using materials readily available to you. In a survival situation, you may quickly have to use an object for something other than its original purpose.

For example, the stack of zip ties in the computer lab used for organizing electrical cords, may now be used to help hold doors closed from the looming zombie corpses that are overtaking you. The shovel that is sitting in the janitor's closet for snow removal is now an advanced piece of weaponry for defeating the undead.

With constant budget cuts at local, state, and federal levels the need to become more resourceful is critical. This is where you are going to have to get creative and start looking at the resources around you for more than what they seem at face value.

Let's take a brief moment to review some of the "big ticket" items that come to mind when you are thinking of valuable resources. Remember, we are fighting for our educational lives and in most cases our personal sanity! Dig deep and be willing to humble yourself and do whatever needs to be done to support your cause. In return you will ultimately be supporting your student's success!

Support Staff

One major problem I think everyone faces is a lack of support staff. As the hands "from the grave" keep increasing the "hands on deck" are quickly decreasing. This means you are having more and more zombies "limping" and "clawing" their way toward you, and the people you have to help combat those educational zombies are less and less each school year, and in some instances, they are decreasing by the day.

When this problem starts to happen, it will likely result in one of two ways. The first outcome is one that will add more stress and zombie related problems to the organization. That outcome is to assume the problem will take care of itself. Most of the time this is something that is out of the control of the classroom teacher's hands. This is where school leadership really needs to step in and prove they are a part of the alliance. To show they are just not a part, but a valued resource. So often though, this is not the case.

For example, many times teachers will lose their planning period because the co-curricular teacher is absent, and no substitute is available to cover them. If it would happen to be your day for your students to receive that co-curricular class, then you are out of luck...you have lost what we referred to earlier as a critical part of your day.

Other examples include having a janitor out for the day resulting in a dirty facility, a cook absent from the lunch line causing increased tension while trying to serve students, an instructional aide for a primary class is home sick leaving a classroom filled with many students who need additional support to the teacher, or maybe the special education teacher is asked to cover for a co-worker who had to leave immediately due to an illness. The list of potential problems could go on for pages.

I am confident each of you reading this are all thinking of similar situations that have happened in your organization. It goes without saying the first outcome of a lack of support staff is a weakened people, which weakens the organization, which weakens your ability to "fight", which allows for the educational zombies to start taking over!

The second outcome is one that eases the burden but requires much more thought and work on the part of the administration. For those principals and other administrative staff reading this, my intention is to not make you look or feel bad. Teachers and other professionals, I ask that you not be overly critical of your own school or district's leadership as a result of my words. No one really knows what another person is going through or dealing with so please keep that in mind as we go forward. I feel the best way to approach this section is to share some personal experiences.

As a school leader, I learned very quickly if I did not intervene in some critical areas my staff was not only going to be overtaken by zombies, they were going to view me as a very weak and uncaring leader. Now, when I say I learned quickly, I am not saying I had some great epiphany one night and the very next day I was a different leader. It actually took me about an entire school year and most of a summer break before I really started to see the light. When I did see the light, it sure was bright!

I'll start by saying as each year passes, the amount of support staff that works at my school fades away due to job advancements and retirements. Unfortunately very few, if any, are ever replaced. In addition, the amount of people available to substitute teach whenever regular staff is absent is also dwindling. This is when the administrative staff needs to step up by stepping in!

In my opinion, there is nothing wrong with a principal covering a few classes from time to time. It would be safe to say that in addition to my regular "principal" duties, I have covered a class for an unfilled absence or someone leaving early at least once per week for the past several years. I actually made a statement once in regards to job titles. What I said was that everyone in an organization in a time of limited resources has to assume nearly every title at some point.

As the principal, I have cleaned up where a child has gotten sick, covered every grade level at one point or another when a substitute was unavailable, served food in the kitchen, stripped and waxed floors, painted halls and classrooms, pulled weeds, assembled furniture, built countertops for a computer lab, raked grass, un-clogged toilets, cleaned up classroom flooding from busted water pipes, spent the night in my office to "babysit" a heat pump on its last legs to prevent frozen water lines, removed live birds and snakes from the hallways, painted murals in the library, gym, and classrooms, supervised field trips, and much more in addition to my regular "principal duties". I don't say these things to be recognized or to receive praise. I say them because they are things that needed to be done, and with limited resources would not have been accomplished!

I'll never forget one Sunday afternoon I was in my school mopping the hallway floors. It just so happened that there was at least one other crazy person also at work on a Sunday (I know, I know...I was not following my advice from the "Rest Up" chapter.) That person asked me why I was mopping the halls. I looked up and smiled and said, "Because they are dirty of course." We ALL have to be teachers, principals, aides, cooks, copy makers, secretaries, and janitors. When we each get involved and share responsibilities, I believe there will be a greater appreciation for each other. Everyone needs to work toward a common goal, the big picture. In doing so we will be more successful as an organization. Staff at my school always go the extra mile and that is what has made us so successful!

Parents and Community Stakeholders

At times we need to look beyond the school system resources for help. Some of those outside resources are not necessarily the norm but still provide much-needed support and assistance. Let's discuss a few examples.

One of your most valuable and often least sought-after resources are parents. Now I know what everyone is thinking at this exact moment. You probably are envisioning "that parent". Most of you would rather have your flesh eaten off before you allow them access to your classroom. I won't disagree that there are often times when "less is more" and you can have "addition by subtraction" when it comes to help in the classroom. Although, if you each would take just a moment, I am sure you can think of some people who have helped you out in a time of need.

Utilizing parents as a resource does not always mean you are recruiting them as a volunteer in the classroom. Maybe they help out in regards to additional supplies, resources, or experiences you may be lacking. One example is networking with professionals that can come in and teach content as a guest speaker. Another obvious approach is really encouraging the parents of your students to become engaged with the content. Allow the parents of your pupils to see the importance of discussing, reading, and reinforcing the content you taught in the classroom each evening at home. The sky really is the limit when you get on a good relationship path with your invested parents.

Along with utilizing parents as resources, you also need to consider your community stakeholders. This can include business professionals, local elected officials, and extended families of your students. When you really start to reach out and make connections with people around your community, you are going to see some light start coming into focus in this dark educational apocalypse.

I know of several instances from both a teacher and leader viewpoint where community stakeholders brought a lot to the table for the organization that I was a part of. I would be almost ashamed to think of all the donations, guest speakers, and field trips that have been made possible because of outside community stakeholders. They were able to provide these opportunities because one simple thing happened. They were asked to help!

Being resourceful is not only about using things around you to serve multiple purposes, it is also about seeing the benefits of those resources. If you have such a prideful heart that it makes you reluctant to ask for help, you are doing not only yourself, but your entire organization a disservice. You will never know the answer until you ask. When it comes to the world of education, you are often told yes more than you are told no by those invested members of the community.

Grants

In addition to parents and other stakeholders, a very commonly overlooked resource is grants. There are literally hundreds of grants available to teachers, ranging from basic grants which award often times in the ballpark of fifty to one hundred dollars and then there are much larger grants which will award thousands of dollars to the recipient. A quick search on the internet will result in a multitude of options. I would also advise that you find some of those "veteran" alliance members, and ask them for input. They may know of an opportunity that is a well-kept secret within the school, district, or community.

The greatest thing about grants is that they are FREE. The worst thing about grants is that they are FREE. What I am trying to say is that very seldom will you be awarded money that does not have strings attached. Keep in mind the amount of money a grant awards is often in direct correlation to the number of strings attached to the funding. For instance, a large grant opportunity will likely result in a lot of paperwork and data collection, whereas smaller grants are often awarded based upon something as basic as an essay.

So, receiving free money is good, but treat it as you would that abandoned grocery store when you are searching for food in an actual apocalypse. Tread carefully and always be on the watch out for a half-dead corpse lying in an inconspicuous place just waiting to get a quick bite out of you. The last thing you want during an educational apocalypse is receiving a "gift" that you thought was going to make it better, actually ending up making it much worse.

Survival Summary:

- Be creative...try to see resources for more than just what they appear at face value.
- Educational support staff are critical...appreciate and utilize them.
- Look to your most invested parents for support.
- Community stakeholders are often willing to assist...create a list of invested stakeholders and start reaching out to them.
- Research grants so you know the requirements before accepting the reward.

Dead Discussion:

1. What are some resources you could utilize better/differently?
2. What are some identified areas of need in your district, school, or classroom? How will you address those needs?
3. Have there been resources used in the past that are no longer being utilized? How could you get those resources back?

-Stay on Course-

In the recent days you have had to deal with various enemies. Some have been more "zombie" in nature while others, sadly enough, still take on the human form. They all have come up against you to destroy what you are trying to accomplish. You chuckle at the thought of their attacks. They have been so unsuccessful. Each time they have tried to penetrate your "camp", your "community", they have been met with a strong section of your defensive barrier, your fence! The fence you have built to help protect your alliance is serving its purpose well. It is keeping those who seek you harm at bay. Even though you take satisfaction in the recent victories, you still realize there is work that needs to be done. You still need to extend portions of your barrier to some of the unguarded sides of your camp. You think about the process you went through to ensure such a safety structure, and you swell with pride. You look at the worn sheet of paper you have had placed on your desk for many months now. You get an urge of excitement as you see the lines crossed through various items that appear on your sheet. Each item marked off is because a section of fence has been completed. You recite the marked off items in your mind, "Updated pacing guide, standards-based assessments, quality lessons, district professional development, and parent contact/communication log". A smile crosses your face. Even though you have more sections of fence to start working on, these sections listed are securely built!

What is one of the first things you would do during a zombie apocalypse if you wanted to protect your community? Some may say collect weapons, gather food, build an alliance, or rest when you can. Of course, all of those things are important (and have been addressed in this

book) but we are talking about the point when all those things are pretty much squared away. We are now talking about when you have found that perfect spot to start having a thriving community again. That critical moment when you are tired of the running and you are determined to "settle new ground". So, I ask again, what would you do to help protect your community?

My mind automatically travels a long way back to those wintery snow days of my childhood. I am referring to the type of eastern Kentucky day following several inches of snow where the sun would be shining and the recipe for the perfect snowball was being prepared. If you were raised in an area with snow, you should know that no true snowball fight should occur without first having a snow fort!

The fort offered you protection from the onslaught of snowballs that were being hurled toward your face. Now in this apocalyptic world, you want to start to build a fort around your community. The fort would consist of a huge fence that followed the perimeter of the area you are trying to protect.

Now I ask you another question, how many farmers or livestock owners do we have out there? If you answered, "Me, I'm one!" You would know the best way to build a fence that is straight and solid, is to look at an immovable point off in the distance like a tree or mountain, and then start setting your fence posts in line with that immovable focal point. By doing this you are staying on course! You are ensuring a well-built fence that will keep those you want to protect "in" and those you are avoiding "out".

Go Straight Forward

Going straight forward when building a fence is a must! It is made possible because you stay in line with an immovable focal point off in the distance. When you are having a difficult time and can hear the fingernails of the undead scratching against the doors trying to overtake you, keep that focal point in mind! You need to understand the big picture. Know what you are trying to achieve and stay on course to accomplish the goal. In high school I was an avid runner. I loved it. I studied what it took to be a good runner. I developed routines and procedures to improve my skills. Do you want to know what the greatest piece of advice I was ever given to improve my running? It was to run tall and look straight forward.

You see the finish line in a race never changes. The goal is always going to be the same. That is not to say that I would not face hardships along the race. I knew, off in the distance was a goal that could and would be reached as long I continued to go forward with all my power and strength. I took confidence in the fact that the goal was immovable.

So many times, when we are facing those difficult moments in education, it is because the journey is hard. The educational undead surrounds us and many of the living have developed a hatred for each other. The days seem bleak and you are forced to deal with hardships (student behaviors, poor resources, etc.) just like I had to deal with hardships in those track and field races so many years ago. Those hardships have been mentioned and will be discussed further as you read because the fact is, they are real!

I don't expect anyone reading this book actually believes in an undead take over, but I have a strong faith that each of you believe in the *educational* undead. The educational undead are the problems that arise due to things out of your control such as family situations, home life, legislative changes, leadership downfalls, poor technology, bad infrastructure, reduction in support staff, budgeting problems and deplorable facilities. Amongst all those problems, don't lose sight of the goal. Stay on course toward your focal point! The focal point, which is your goal, could include a variety of things. Some common goals that come to mind would be increased student achievement, more engaged lesson, personal growth through professional learning, or better communication processes with parents. Chip away little by little to see your students grow, and as a result you will see yourself grow professionally as well!

Goals Don't Move-They Change

As we reach the mid-point of the, "Stay on Course" chapter I would like to answer some possible questions you may have. You may be wanting to ask something along these lines, "Woody, you have said you need to stay on course and keep in line with an immovable focal point off in the distance. That is all fine and good if you are building one continuous straight fort wall or fence. Don't you need to surround the entire educational community? Don't the sections of fence need to connect back to the other sections? What happens when you change directions?"

These questions are valid! For the fence builders out there, you know at some point you have to change directions to have a fence that surrounds all your livestock. My answer to these questions are very simplistic. You set a corner post-then you change directions! Think about that "turn" or "corner post" in your fence as a milestone. You have stayed on course and in line with the end goal ahead of you, your focal point. Your fence is strong and safe. You have made progress and are protecting your educational alliance. Now you have to change directions. At that point what you do is easy. As you turn your body and you start out on that new course you find the new immovable point, a new goal. You locate it and then start off again working toward that goal.

You see, your goals do not move. They may give the appearance sometimes of moving, but the fact is they are actually new goals. For example, let's say you want to receive a certain "score title" based upon your states standardized testing model. I am not a big proponent of standardized testing, but the fact of the matter is standardized testing is a part of our educational world and everyone *should* want to be as successful as possible according to it.

As a result of all of your efforts as an organization, you are able to see your goal met! You have reached the status symbol you were working for! Congratulations! Do you stop building the fence? No! You set a strong corner post, you make a "turn", locate that NEW immovable focal point (goal) off in the distance and then stay on course to meet that goal. This process will repeat itself at every turn you make. Just like a literal fence, your figurative fence will have small posts (objectives) along the way. These are the small steps you take along your path before you set that huge corner post! Each objective along the way needs to be celebrated. With each small post (objective) you set (accomplish) you need to celebrate! These small celebrations of victory will give you the much-needed momentum to continue on!

Always remember when you meet your main goal, you set a strong corner post and celebrate even more! Then locate a new goal off in the distance, use that goal as your new focal point, stay on course, set small posts along the way with mini celebrations, reach the goal, set a strong corner post, celebrate, make a turn, and REPEAT. Keep doing this until you have your entire educational community surrounded and protected.

You now may ask a very short and basic question, "So what happens when all of your educational goals are met and your fence has successfully wrapped around to fully surround your educational community and alliance?" This is where you then branch out to find a new community (educational area to protect) and start building a fence to protect that area based upon a new set of goals and criteria.

Repair Breaches in Your Defense

No matter how well you have built the fence that surrounds your community, there will always be a need for repairs. Earlier we discussed each focal point that you used to guide your figurative fence was a "goal". What we did not discuss was the vast variety of goals that appear in our educational world. We touched upon state assessment and "titles" of accomplishment that may be associated with those scores as a goal. But that is just one goal. That entire fence you are building to protect your community will have many small posts (objectives) and corner posts (overall goals) throughout.

Different organizations may have different goals or they may have the same goals but in a different order. There is nothing wrong with that. What is needed to be accomplished at one organization early on in the educational community protection process, may be something that is already established or not as important to another organization.

Here are some of the goals that come to mind for me. As a school leader, I will be the first to admit I have not successfully reached these goals. These are the areas I have focused on, and will continue to do so.

Let's take a look at some of my goals. In addition to wanting to be successful on state assessments, I think about: quality student engagement in every classroom, an efficient process for determining student referrals/retention, an effective school-wide RTI plan, teacher collaboration, relationship building (teacher to teacher, teacher to student, student to student, student to administration, teacher to parent, teacher to administration, school to community, school to central office staff...the combinations could go on and on), consistent management of behavior, fair evaluation process for teachers, clear communication plan, leadership opportunities for both staff and students, manageable curriculum design, streamlined data collection process, and a common sense approach to monitoring instruction to just name a few.

As you accomplish each goal, you then move to the next goal. Although, that does not mean you never come back and revisit the "section of the fence" you just completed. Just like a literal fence, your figurative fence will take on structural damage from time to time. If the damage is not assessed and corrected, the breach in that section of fence will get larger and larger. It makes no difference that the rest of the fence from that point forward is strong and secure, because you have a weak point. The now weakened area of fence will allow the educational zombie forces and other educational enemies to penetrate your defense!

Think of your damaged fence like a chain with a weak link. The weak link is eventually going to break rendering the rest of the chain useless. The defensive educational barrier you are building is no different. That is why you must do what I refer to as "walking the fence".

When I was younger, I was exposed to a whole host of critters that were kept in a fenced-in enclosure on my farm. Often times that fenced-in area enclosed several acres. Living on somewhat of a menagerie, I would have animals such as coyotes, foxes, horses, cattle, pigs, goats, and even whitetail deer in these rather large areas. I had to religiously "walk the fence" of these enclosures to search for areas that had been damaged by storms, flooding, disrespectful humans, and even the animals themselves.

When I came upon an area of the fence that had been destroyed, I set out to repair the breach. This was an ongoing and never-ending process. Even now that I am much older and have several fewer animals to care for, my system has not changed. My process of "fence walking" still goes on today!

Our educational fence that is comprised of multiple objectives and goals is no different. If you want to keep your community safe, and the entire protective barrier effective, you have to "walk your fence"! You will need to revisit past goals to make sure they are still solid and mend the breaches as they come up.

For example, a part of your educational fence may be made up of "a clear communication plan". You have come up with a thoughtful system of communicating with all stakeholders and have put your plan into action. You follow your plan with extreme fidelity for a solid school year. As a result of your efforts, you witness great benefits. You are able to keep multiple educational zombies at bay. You feel like you, your alliance, and the educational community you are protecting with your strong fence is safe. There is not a feeling much greater than that comfort, especially in a time that can be so desolate. You should feel proud and successful!

The next school year is now upon you and you decide to work on a new goal, for example, a streamlined data collection process, which is the prudent thing to do if you want to continue to go forward. As you work on this new goal in making the data collection process smooth and effective you discontinue your efforts on your clear communication plan. This is where you now have a breach in your fence! You have allowed your mind to advance to a new goal, which is wonderful, but you have done that advancement while sacrificing the continued work of a past goal. As a result, you now have a breach in your defense. You have allowed an opportunity for the educational zombies or other enemies to attack!

Staying on course and establishing new goals is amazing and something all great teachers should do. What separates those great teachers from the truly amazing teachers is "fence walking"! The teachers that can move forward, while continually addressing and ensuring past accomplishments do not fail, are the ones that will survive an educational zombie apocalypse. When all the zombies in your school life are defeated, the dust from the battlefield has settled, and the world is starting to come back into view, those teachers will be the ones that will rebuild in the new era. The "fence walking" is a critical key in overcoming the educational undead!

Survival Summary:

- Always push forward and stay on course.
- Build a protective barrier based on a variety of goals.
- Goals don't move-they change!
- Once you reach small steps and big goals be sure to celebrate those accomplishments.
- Repeat the process of reaching new goals until your entire "educational community" is protected.
- Always "walk your fence" searching for damaged sections in need of repair.
- After your protective barrier is complete, find a *new* area to establish a *new* community and start the process over.

Dead Discussion:

1. What are the major "focal points" (goals) for your district, school, or classroom?
2. What objectives (small fence posts) have been set forth to reach those goals?
3. How do/can you celebrate after you reach an objective and goal?
4. What system do you have in place for "fence walking"?

-Fight or Flight-

You have prepared for months and the time has finally come…it is time for the ultimate zombie battle! A battle that cannot be avoided! As you look out to your troops you see them sitting quietly, they are awaiting their next set of instructions. Each one is equipped with an advanced piece of weaponry. Although, what they hold is only around six inches long, it will be a critical component in the upcoming battle. Each "weapon" has been sharpened to a point that would embarrass most swords. On your command the troops take off to fight. As the battle rages on, minute by minute many look to you as their general, their leader. You see sweat pouring from the brows of some, others have tears forming in their eyes, while the rest are feverishly attacking their enemy with great tenacity. You have told them many times that you will not be able to help them in this particular zombie war. You can only move throughout the battlefield silently. As weapons dull or break you quickly replace them with fresh ones from your stockpile…that will be their only assistance from you. This battle is predicted to wage on for sixty minutes and not a second longer. While making your rounds you hear an alarm go off. Your mind quickly engages your mouth and you shout, "TIME! Pencils down. This concludes Part A of this year's Reading Standardized Test. We will take a short break and resume Part B when we return."

Something I heard numerous times early on in my career as both a teacher and administrator is that I needed to understand the times to fight and the times for flight. I was told that I needed to make a choice between "having school" and having an argument when situations occurred. I learned very quickly I would often choose to "have school" versus fighting over every little thing. I would give the same advice to those who are reading this.

In most cases, it is going to be much better for you and the students you care for if you just leave some situations alone. Don't get sucked down in a negative pit of despair by others. This concept goes together seamlessly with staying on course. Let's take a few moments to discuss fight or flight in more detail.

Fight

I am a firm believer that you must stand up for what is right! The problem is that many times people have different views of right and wrong. The important thing is that you must be able to distinguish between those differences and then go with what is truly right every time.

This means that sometimes you are going to have to respectfully disagree with people. The key word here is respectfully. Disagreeing with someone does not mean you have to be rude, actually you need to do it while being "nice". Being nice doesn't mean you have to compromise your values. Being humble and meek does not mean you are going to stumble and be weak. It means you are going to have a calm and gentle nature about you, it means you are going to "be nice." If it comes to a point that you feel like you can no longer be nice then you may have to fight...nicely.

The same goes for when you encounter the really tough times during your educational career. I would encourage you to be nice at all cost, but sometimes you are going to have to fight back. As a teacher, you may be told something that you know really isn't in the best interest of your students. Poor guidance is an example of an educational zombie. It is during these times, you have to respectfully "fight" back and share your concerns. I am not advocating for anyone to be insubordinate (that will get you fired) but you have to know how to voice the concerns you have regarding the decisions being made for you and your students.

Oftentimes principals and administrative staff want to offer "guidance" or give "expectations" to teachers without really understanding what it is like to be in that teacher's shoes. Later, you will read about the first two things I quickly learned about being a school principal. One of those lessons learned was that you cannot "pull the wool" over the eyes of your teachers. Meaning, teachers SHOULD NOT be treated in a way that makes them seem....well....stupid if you want to be frank!

Administrators should be exposed to the classroom environment thoroughly, consult and collect preliminary data and information before offering suggestions and telling teachers how to run their class. Would you want a surgeon to start cutting and working on your body without first doing some preliminary testing, consulting with your family doctor, or reviewing past medical records? Of course not! You need to know that fighting for what is right is perfectly okay. If done correctly you will gain respect both with peers and your leadership. Your feedback may be ignored, and you may be instructed to go ahead and do what you were originally told, even after you voiced your concerns. If this is the case, take comfort in the fact that at least you can say you advocated for what you felt was right in your heart. Just because something is not corrected this time that does not mean the next time there is a concern you will be ignored.

Trust me, as a school leader, I have had many occasions where I wish I would have listened more to my staff. I have had times where I did not heed the advice of others that I lead, and it has come back to bite me, no zombie pun intended. So, what did I do? I humbled myself, ate some "crow", tucked my tail between my legs and apologized to that staff member. The next time that staff member offered a suggestion, I was much more apt to listen and take their advice. Did I lose credibility by not listening the first time? Maybe, some. Did I lose more credibility when I apologized? No, that was the first step in gaining it back. Was I viewed as a weak and indecisive leader the next time a situation came up and I asked that same teacher for their opinion? I don't think so. In actuality, I think at that point I was viewed as a more effective leader than before, because I learned from my mistake and sought out their professional advice and guidance. I recognized them as a thoughtful individual with leadership qualities. I showed that I valued their perspective. The main take away from this fight section would be to pick the battles that you feel will make the greatest lasting impact on student achievement. Even if you lose the battle, you can say it was at least worth fighting for.

Flight

I know this concept may be very difficult for many of you. I will tell you why I think that. If you are reading this book, more than likely you are the type of person that I would refer to as intrinsically motivated. You are someone that seeks out new paths to better yourself. You are a leader in your organization or will be very shortly. You are not afraid to get your hands dirty and understand that hard work does and will pay off. With that said, you are also possibly the type of person who does not want to back down from a fight. I can relate to you.

I hate being pressured or feeling trapped. I don't ever want to be backed into a corner. Even when I eat at a restaurant, I refuse to have my back turned to the exits, because I want to be able to see who is coming in and who is going out. (You may be thinking, *"Now, the whole "no back turned to an exit" is a little extreme."* I blame that complex on the westerns I have read in my lifetime.) The point I am trying to make is that there is a strong possibility you and I are very similar individuals. When we are pressured to a certain point, we are going to feel the need to "fight" back. As mentioned before, if the issues pushing your buttons are going to have a negative impact on the lives of children, you really need to stand up and take on that battle (but remember, "be nice"). If the issue is something mundane, don't get yourself all worked up over the small things.

I have come to a realization that many of these small "bites" and "scratches" from the zombies that are present in your educational apocalypse are just mere distractions. I believe that many of the enemies we discussed earlier on pick these little fights to avoid working on what is really needed. My father always referred to this as people who work harder to get out of work instead of just working hard.

For example, let's say your principal has forgotten to inform the staff that there is going to be a schoolwide assembly. You will have many staff members that make the adjustment in the schedule and "go with the flow" when they receive the information the morning of. You may have others who really want to tear the principal apart because now they will be "so far behind". As a result of the assembly, they will now have to edit plans for the next several days, which will then make them late turning in assessment data or some other required document. Those staff members may even come to you and try to entice you to join the fight. This is a time to just step away.

Sure, the principal should have communicated things better to make it easier for staff to plan out the day, but the fact is mistakes happen. This my friends is not an example of a life-altering mistake. Let's say you are reading this and you are a principal. I can hear the cheers now. "Yeah, it was not that big of a deal, let's give the principal a break." What if the shoe were on the other foot? How many times do teachers get overwhelmed and miss a deadline, then administrators want to really get upset? What I am saying is that we all mess up daily. Every little mistake or miscommunication should not elicit an all-out brawl. This is a time for flight!

One thing I always like to discuss when talking with my supervisors, as well as my employees, is that we need to focus on big picture things. Remember when we talked about those immovable objects off in the distance? We should set our eyes toward those big goals when building our fence to keep out the educational undead! That unmovable focal point is the big picture. Many people want to fight to pull away from the big picture. Don't let it happen! Don't be distracted by things that serve no true purpose.

In education, you are going to be asked to deal with many undead bodies creeping your way. We have mentioned them so much that you should be able to list them off in a hurry. A huge percent of your educational zombies are things out of your control like compliance training, mundane meetings that serve no purpose, students coming from bad home situations and legislative rulings that impact your future. Don't waste your energy on fighting battles you cannot win! Control the things that you can control!

Survival Summary:

- Know the difference between FIGHT and FLIGHT!
- When you feel the need to "fight" do it respectfully.
- Even if your suggestions are not taken, do not let that stop you from offering more suggestions in the future.
- When dealing with the small things just take "flight"....walk away.
- Don't engage in negative behaviors or waste energy.
- Focus on what you can CONTROL, not what you can't.

Dead Discussion:

1. What "zombie battles" are you willing to fight? In what "zombie battles" are you willing to take flight?
2. In what ways will you prepare for those battles you feel like you will need to fight?

-Wear Protective Armor-

If you have learned anything about battling the undead in this "apocalypse", it is that you better have some good armor. The bites and scratches never stop coming at you, and often times in all directions. As you look in the mirror, you met your reflection's piercing gaze, your own gaze! You tell yourself that your training has prepared you for all types of enemies. Your past experiences assure you that you will not fall in battle! You apply another layer of "war paint" to your face. You pay close attention to the areas under your eyes. Even though you are tired, there is no need for the dark circles that lie beneath them to let everyone else know it. As you make your way to your transport vehicle, you swiftly grab the steaming dark cup of liquid that is sitting on the counter by your personal food pantry. You take a quick sip, you realize as the smooth, rich liquid makes it way down your throat that this beverage serves as a special piece of armor all in itself. You imagine the hot drink wrapping your soul in a protective cocoon. As you start your engine, you take a quick glance into your rearview mirror and give a slight nod. You seem satisfied with your hair and the makeup you have chosen today. You then place your large mug of coffee in the cup holder, place your car in reverse, and start your journey to school.

Just in case you missed the Ninja Turtle reference I made earlier; I will insert another one here. When I was a very young man, I walked up to my father while hunching over and said, "Dad, feel my back." After he took his rather large paw and did a few massage motions over my back and upper shoulders he said, "Wow! Your back is really getting hard!" He was assuming that I was referring to my muscles getting stronger and hardened as most young boys do. He was wrong.

Me being the true lover of all things Ninja Turtle replied, "I knew it! I'm turning into a turtle!" Turtle being pronounced tool-tle as a result of a slight "r" speech impediment. You see, I thought I was growing a shell. Now I ask, what is the purpose for a turtle shell? The answer is easy, to protect!

Throughout history, anytime an army has been asked to go into battle, they would be equipped with some level of protection. Protective armor has evolved over the years from chain mail and steel breastplates to high tech, lightweight Kevlar body suits. The protective armor you put on in the academic setting to defeat the zombie mobs, and other enemies that are present during your educational apocalypse is no different.

Physical Body

One thing I have learned during my years in education, is that most people get sick pretty easily when they are first starting out. It is hard to do basic tasks when you don't feel good, let alone be an active contributor to the education of the young people you teach and lead. The point here is simple, but hard to swallow, because many of us deal with this problem. We do not take good care of our bodies. I am not judging; I am speaking from my own personal life.

Before I became a school principal, I was a physical education and health teacher. Before that, I was an athlete in high school running miles a day and playing basketball from dawn to dusk. When I walked through the front doors of the school I am now working at for my interview, I weighed a nice 203 lbs. I know that may seem heavy but on a good day I stand about 6'1", but am built thick through the chest and shoulders, so that was not a bad weight for me. I was offered the position one week after my interview and graciously accepted. With each passing year, I have become less active. As the stresses of the job increased, so did the number on my scales. Like many of you reading this, I began having not what I would call a "full apocalyptic year", but I would have small educational zombie hordes that had to be defeated rather quickly from time to time.

Then it happened. I was pumping gas at around 6:45 am one morning at a local fueling station. As I walked toward the entrance to pay, I started feeling a pain in my chest. At first, it was light, but as I took each step it became more severe and every time my foot would hit the pavement it felt as sharp needles were piercing my entire upper body. I called my father who was about fifteen miles away and told him I was experiencing some chest pain. He immediately told me he was calling the local ambulance. Then I called my mother who was working only about three miles down the road and told her an ambulance was in route, but she needed to come to get me quick because I was having extreme discomfort in my chest. A sensation I had never felt!

With the pain coming in short waves, I was able to get in my car and pull away from the gas pump to a small grocery store parking lot that joined the fueling station. This local grocery store has an inside pizza carry out station. It is one of the few places in the entire county that you can get a delivery style pizza. It is frequented often by many of the residents. You may be wondering how the pizza shop factors into the story.

Well, the entire time I was waiting for my mother or ambulance (whoever arrived first to pick me up) I could not help but think to myself, *Here I am in the middle of this parking lot and I am going to die of a massive heart attack.* Then I started thinking, *Every time someone comes to buy a pizza they are going to say, "Well here is where ole Woody died. Right here where we are picking up our Friday night dinner."* That thought alone, was enough to drive me crazy!

So, to make a fairly long story much shorter, my mother did arrive and rushed me to the hospital embarrassing any professional race car driver with her hill flattening and curve straightening speed. Once in the emergency room, multiple medical tests were administered and everything came back "clean". Even though I was not diagnosed with a heart attack (which I was beyond thankful for) I was "woke up" enough to realize that I needed to make some major changes in regards to my health.

You see, my time in school that year was not that bad. I was coming off back to back years of the highest test scores in the school's history. We received multiple awards and recognition at the state level. I was only in my fourth year of administration and only my tenth year in education. I was hitting my stride so to speak but I had packed on about sixty pounds above that 203 that I mentioned earlier and I was not taking care of myself.

I am now on a better track but it is a daily struggle. When I get discouraged, I try to lift myself up with a very simple thought, *We all have zombies around us. Some more than others. Why in the world should we add to our own difficulties by not being more mindful of our own health?* My father has one very simple piece of parenting advice that he gives me and other people that he counsels. "Give your kids a fighting chance in life."

What he means is, you as a parent need to instruct and lead them in a way that is morally and ethically right so that they can at least have a basic understanding of Godly principles. Taking care of your physical body, is you giving *yourself* that fighting chance to keep taking on the stresses of your school year and to overcome them.

Credibility

Earlier I mentioned the first two lessons I learned as an administrator. The first lesson I learned about being a school principal is that I did not know a thing about being a school principal. I think this comment rings true for most of us when we start an unfamiliar position. I always then follow up quickly with the second thing I learned about being a school principal, and that is you cannot "pull the wool" over the eyes of your teachers and staff. Both of these quick lessons apply to a critical piece of armor which is credibility. Credibility, much like someone's reputation, is very hard to gain but can be lost rather quickly.

Having a high level of credibility is different than being "liked". Often times, people in your life will find you to be a credible individual but may not enjoy being around you at all. Having credibility ensures that your staff or students are going to take what you say as the truth. They are going to follow your lead because you have proven yourself time and time again. You are like an army general, who is battle-tested and have gained approval not by the voice of men but with the scars on your educational body. Having credibility is like having on thick forearm guards. Those protective pieces of equipment allow you to go amidst the herds of the educational undead and sustain bite after bite to your arms that never penetrate your flesh. Just as those forearm guards protect one of the most commonly attacked places on your physical body, your credibility protects your educational body.

Now, I propose a question. What do you feel is your current level of credibility? Many of the questions that are asked throughout this reading are simple and straightforward. This is not the case with this inquiry. Here you really need to be self-reflective and evaluate how others view you. Once again, this is not an assessment of your "likeability", rather it is a view if you have the skills to perform your job proficiently.

I would predict at this point you have basically answered this question one of three ways. First, you have stated confidently that you have a high level of credibility, and you have the track record to prove it. If that truly is the case, then I applaud you and with a hearty pat on the back and send you on your way to keep fighting the educational undead. The second way I would have guessed you to respond, is that you feel in some areas of your profession you are viewed as a highly credible individual. In other areas though, you understand and accept your weaknesses and know that if you are put in a particular situation you would not feel adequate to take on the task. My third prediction of your potential answer is that you simply feel like you are lost to all aspects of your job. You believe if there is not an imminent intervention you will be joining the zombie mob, because you can already feel the breath of the undead upon your skin. You fear that teeth are about to follow! What happens when you are overtaken and bit? You *turn*! You join the very forces that you once were fighting against.

Let's take a moment to focus on the last two answers I predicted. Both deal with you, to some degree, feeling like you are not a credible resource. I would dare say if you have taken the time to read this book you are on the right path to fixing that problem. I too, at different points in my career, have felt like I had not gained or had possibly lost some credibility. You lose credibility by discussing, making decisions, or by having expectations of people that for lack of a better word are ridiculous. When I say ridiculous that encompasses a whole host of things.

For one, it means that you are trying to involve yourself in areas, and are expecting people to follow your leadership in those areas, when you yourself have no clear understanding. If you are in the "fake it until you can make it" phase I would advise with great caution that you do not take on tasks you have no understanding about.

So many times, in education, we are forced to start new initiatives with no clear goal or ending expectation. How many times have we all heard that dreaded phrase, "We are building this plane as we fly it." To me, that is one of the most ignorant sayings ever. I ask you this, how many of you would actually step foot on a literal airplane that is unfinished and take off three thousand feet above the ground? None of you! These types of things will cause you to lose your credibility, or keep you from gaining it so fast you will be forever trying to battle back. Avoid them at all cost!

So that was the negative side of the credibility equation. This is just a snapshot of an instance that could cause you to lose credibility or to keep you from gaining it. For every negative that is discussed, there has to be a positive. Good coaches point out issues in their athletes that need to be improved, but then go the extra mile to help them in those improvements.

So how do you gain initial or lost credibility? The easiest thing I have learned is to obtain as much knowledge and understanding of a concept before you present it to others. For a teacher, this is as basic as understanding the standards that you teach. For administrators, an example would be making sure you're knowledgeable about what your teachers are being expected to do. As a principal, it is important for me to be able to talk competently to my staff as well as supervisors about the day to day operation of my school. This involves everything from books (academics), to beans (food services), to ball (athletics). Have I always been able to discuss these various factions of education? No! I had to involve myself every day in all facets of the school. I did this by speaking with my coaches, serving food in the lunch line, and most importantly by being in classrooms. Now, when I say I get in classrooms I am not talking about conducting typical "walkthroughs" where I would sit and record what the teacher is doing, take notes on how they need to improve or provide tons of feedback on instructional practices. No, I will go in, move around, listen to kids talk and discuss concepts, and watch the teacher engage in amazing teaching. I ask kids if they need help and try to be a blessing versus a hindrance. The entire time this is going on I am able to know exactly who is doing well, who is struggling, and what standards are being taught.

As a teacher you can follow the same method. Get involved in the learning process. Have the deepest and best understanding of the standards you teach. Follow other educators on social media platforms. Watch videos or observe other classrooms. The main thing is to surround yourself with quality content related to your profession.

Listen, I tried the first approach, the "build the plane as you fly it", it did not go over too well. No pun intended. My first year as a head administrator (now remember what I learned first about being an administrator from earlier) I conducted numerous walkthroughs, collected tons of documentation, and reported to my supervisors all the great things I had done. I was then awarded the following fall, when my first year's test data was reported, with an overall **DROP** in school performance!

The scores had declined from the year prior. I took the credit for the drop and contributed much of it to my lack of understanding of how quality walkthroughs, along with other administrative practices should be conducted. What made me even more upset, was when I looked back in the not so distant past and seen another situation that had a similar negative impact!

Let's back up about two years prior before I was blessed with principal position I am describing. At that point in time, I was the itinerant assistant principal at another elementary school and the county high school. Just like in my current position, I was responsible for conducting daily walkthroughs along with other tasks, and providing feedback to teachers. I performed this duty diligently logging in nearly over one hundred walkthroughs per month. I kept copies of all my documentation in a three-ring binder not knowing when it may come in handy. The following summer a principal position was posted in our district. I had always told myself as an assistant, I would apply to any head principal opening that came available, because my ultimate goal was to lead my own school. I was blessed with the opportunity to interview for the position. As many do during an interview, I brought supplemental resources that I thought may aid in the council's decision to hire me. One of those resources was my rather large three-ring binder which was the housing agent for my walkthrough documentation.

To increase the speed of this story I will cut directly to my main point in telling it. I did not receive the principal position for that school. I will never know all the reasons why I was not hired, but as we all do when things don't work out, we have speculations. I am not saying that showing that hiring committee my walkthrough binder was what cost me the job, but I do believe it did not help me.

My point for sharing these two life experiences is simple. I had a belief that the number of walkthroughs was going to outweigh the quality. In doing so it did not only result in a backset in my career, but it also caused me to lose a bit of credibility. That is why now my walkthroughs are conducted on a much different scale, and as a result, I have seen my credibility regained and success rates for both my students and staff go up.

As a teacher you may be faced with similar situations. I am sure you can think of times when you completed tasks that you thought was going to help you, in return, you found out they actually hurt or hindered you! Please evaluate all that you do with your students and fellow staff members. Make sure you have a full knowledge base before you try to go forward teaching or discussing a concept. Everything I am saying does not have to relate to teaching of standards. You need to be able to talk knowledgeably about various areas of education to build an overall credibility.

I would not be at the point in my career now if I had not learned this concept I am discussing. As teachers you need to know exactly what you are wanting to accomplish, and then find the correct path that leads to those accomplishments.

Beginning teachers may face similar problems that I faced as a new principal. I know you won't be conducting walkthroughs but you will be giving feedback, speaking with parents, working with students, and reporting to your supervisors on things that are happening in your classroom. In doing so you can make yourself appear very credible or weak depending on the level of knowledge you have about your job. If you are feeling discouraged or think you have a low credibility rating, you need to meet with your alliance and find a way to take on the undead and see your armor strengthened.

Professional Dress

For those reading this who know me best, I am sure they will get a good hard laugh out of this section. They will laugh because they know I am not the person to be giving anyone fashion advice. The truth is, they are correct! This section is not necessarily about fashion, although I am not against anyone who prides themselves in being fashionable. This section addresses simply looking professional. When I was in my later years of college and had enough credits to substitute teach, you would not find me covering for a teacher without a dress shirt and tie on. The point here is to do as the old saying goes...dress for success!

Dressing professionally does two major things for you as an individual. First, it shows all those around you that you are serious about what you are doing and you don't take your job for granted or lightly. Secondly, you will feel more confident as a person and a professional. Don't take what I am saying the wrong way. I am not advising anyone to go spend thousands or even hundreds of dollars for a new wardrobe. My advice here is to simply look nice and professional. I don't care if your outfit came from a high priced "brand" named store or a department outlet. As long as it reflects the professional nature of the organization you will be well on your way to keeping some zombies away.

One of my favorite things to do as a coach was to get new uniforms for my players. Those new uniforms seemed to actually make the players perform better! How could this be? The athletes felt better about themselves and the other teams took them more seriously. This concept is no different than what I mentioned above. To gain the respect of those around you (administration and students) and to make you feel more confident in your abilities, always take a second look in the mirror and ask yourself if you are going to make an impact with the "armor" you are wearing for this educational zombie battle.

The Environment You Create

We have all been evaluated, to some degree, on the type of environment and culture we create in our classroom. Although I don't agree with all the pieces of various evaluations systems across our nation and world, I will say that I agree with the importance of this topic. I agree because it is something that teachers can control.

Let me explain, teachers can control what type of environment they create or how they react to situations that come up. Teachers cannot control the actions of a student who may have a bad home life and comes to school with a negative attitude day in and day out. They can, however, control their reaction to that student.

When you create a safe place for students and build those precious relationships we have already referred to, you are adding to your protective armor. You will be able to take on more bites and scratches from the various educational zombies because you have layers and layers of protection. I am not saying those bites and scrapes are enjoyable and should be ignored, but at least they can be addressed without overtaking you!

One of the most efficient ways to create a good environment is to gain trust. Once you gain the trust of those you are trying to teach and lead, you have taken the appropriate step in the right direction. The easiest way to gain trust is to simply not lie. If you tell your students you are going to do something, then do it. This can be positive consequences in the form of rewards or this can also mean you stick to negative consequences in the form of punishment. The point here is you do what you say you are going to do.

This simple concept has cost me more than a few dollars over the years. For example, at the start of every basketball season, I would go into our high school boy's basketball locker room. I would tell the players that if anyone slam dunked a ball in a game, I would give that player one hundred dollars cash! For years I never had to pay up, because it never happened. Then the day came. Yes, there was one year where a great athlete came through the system, and he did it. He dunked a basketball during a regulation game. I was not there to witness it but my phone quickly buzzed with a text message that informed me of the event. The text also informed me of my yearly promise. As a result, the next time I saw the young man, I handed him a crisp one-hundred-dollar bill.

In addition to this story, I have had to buy dinners, video game gift cards, books, candy and even clothes for students because I made a promise to them. What would have happened if I did not follow through on those promises? I would have lost my credibility with that student. My relationship would have been broken. The environment, at least for the individual that had been lied too, would no longer be safe. I would then no longer have that layer of protection.

Attitude

When I think about a person's attitude in relation to armor, only one piece comes to mind. The helmet! The helmet's main purpose is to protect not only your head but what lies inside, your brain. Your brain is a powerful tool but it can also work against you if you allow it to be damaged. Having a negative attitude will destroy your mind quickly. I understand that with all the problems we are facing in education today, it is not hard to become negative. You must realize that once you allow yourself to get in that negative state, you have gone to the other side. You are now either that educational zombie trying to overtake others or maybe that rogue human who is exploiting others in a time of uprising and unsettlement. Either way, you are allowing yourself to become part of the problem as opposed to the solution, you have become the very enemy you once were trying to defeat.

When you have a positive attitude, you are able to function and think much clearer. You are not weighed down by the troubles of the looming educational apocalypse, rather you are finding ways to capitalize in times of destruction. Much research has been conducted on the power of positive thinking, and I agree that the power of a positive mindset is beyond measure. As a former athlete and still as a principal I practice visualization. For those unfamiliar with the term, I will explain it briefly. Visualization is basically thinking about something in a positive way and realizing it in the future. I am not saying people can see the future or have psychic abilities, I am saying that when you focus on something, the chances it will work out the way you imagine it are strong.

Having a good attitude is like having a force field around your mind. It protects you from the onslaught of issues that are coming your way on a daily basis. I once heard my father say he was happy that the members of the church were sharing burdens with him and each other. This got me thinking a bit about how sharing a burden relates to having a positive attitude. When you share burdens, you are bringing up issues of concern. On the surface, this sounds a whole lot like complaining but when you look deeper there is a significant contrast in the two.

When a person complains, they are pointing out negative things about the organization, staff, students, or parents but they never really offer any way to help with the problem. This contributes to having a negative attitude, which will ultimately lead to destruction. On the other hand, when you share a burden you are voicing concerns for areas that need to be addressed but you are doing it in a positive manner. You are recognizing there is a situation that needs to be fixed, and you are asking for help, but you are also stating that you are willing to do your part in making the situation better.

Having a good attitude resonates high amongst those you work with, as well as your administrators and students. Every aspect of your job will improve when you stay positive. There is a lot of places on your body that can be attacked and withstand a few bites. Your mind is not one of those places. It must be protected at all cost! Don't let the stresses of your job bring you down to a negative place. Remember that many of the educational zombies and other enemies that you face come from areas that are well beyond your control. Reflect back on the "Fight or Flight" chapter, take on the enemies that are critical for you to reach your goal. If there are adversaries you can avoid, then do so! You will see your attitude strengthen with the high levels of positivity in your life.

I like to compare a good attitude to gold. You don't get either one without overcoming some hardships and trials. Just like gold, your life is going to be put through extreme periods of heat and fire. Through that process, you will become more refined and valuable. You see, when gold is heated, all of the impurities and elements that lower its worth are separated. They collect at the top of the crucible. These impurities are referred to as dross. Once the dross is removed, you are left with pure gold. When you face trials in your life, you too will become more refined. The dross that collects will be removed from your life, leaving you with something very valuable, a positive attitude.

Survival Summary:

- ☣ You need to have multiple pieces of armor to help you withstand the many bites throughout an educational zombie apocalypse.
- ☣ Take care of your physical body...the benefits will reach far beyond your "school life".
- ☣ Gain credibility by understanding all facets of your job.
- ☣ Dress professionally and you will gain increased confidence and others will view your actions as intentional and serious.
- ☣ Create a safe environment through relationship building and gaining trust...if you say you are going to do it, then do it!
- ☣ Maintain a positive attitude...even when things don't look so positive.

Dead Discussion:

1. What are your strongest/weakest "pieces of armor"?
2. What are some ways to improve or add to your existing armor?
3. Do you have alliance members that could help in the process of "forging new armor"?

-It Will Not Last Forever-

*It finally happened! You have been captured. Not by the undead monsters that roam around taking bites out of people, but from another enemy...a more "intelligent" foe. What makes it even worse is that your entire alliance has been taken as well. You all now sit quietly unable to move. The torture that you will endure will exhaust your mental and physical toughness. Perspiration drips from your forehead and you feel moisture under your arms due to the lack of air flow in this confined space. The enemy has you each seated in rows, shoulder to shoulder like livestock. A bright light shines from the center of the room's ceiling, projecting a rather large image on the white surface that you are facing. Words come into focus as the normal room lights are dimmed. A man in the front begins talking. The persecution is about to begin. He hits a button and the image changes; new words appear like magic on the white surface. As the seconds turn to minutes, the words keep changing. You have seen him hit the button fifty times, and it still seems like there is no end in sight! You pick up on small bits of information as he talks. You look to your fellow alliance members and they seem as lost and confused as you are. Finally, you hear the words, "and these will be the new standards for this upcoming year". After what seems like hours, the main lights are turned back on and you shield your eyes from the piercing rays coming from the ceiling. The presenter then says the following, "At this time we will break for a thirty-minute lunch. When we return, we will start building **from scratch** the new curriculum based upon the revised academic standards we just discussed. Don't worry about bringing any of your current materials, none of those will help. I would suggest you get to know each other at lunch. The* *next three days of this summer professional learning will be dedicated to this topic."*

Just like many of the bad things that happen in your life, there will come a point for it to be over. The educational apocalypse that you are facing is no different. Just as all good things must come to an end, we can take assurance in the fact that the bad will as well. Too many times we get tunnel vision on the negative aspects of our job. We only allow ourselves to see the educational zombies, with their gnashing teeth, as opposed to what may lie beyond the undead mob.

Magic Flash Paper

As I referenced earlier, I consider myself a bit of a nerd. So it should come to no surprise when I discuss my interest in magic. I am not saying I am a grand illusionist who wears a black cloak and pulls rabbits out of hats or coins from behind ears. I am saying I have a general interest in the art, and practice close up magic often with young people.

No true close up magician will ever be caught doing a trick without having a very useful tool in their toolbox, flash paper! I will now break the sacred magician's secret code to share with you what flash paper is. It is basically regular paper, although super thin, that has been soaked in a highly flammable solution and then allowed to dry for an extended period of time. I would like to insert a very strong warning here, DO NOT try to create your own flash paper. It is a very cheap prop that can be purchased online easily. With that being said, I use flash paper for a whole host of tricks where I want the paper to vanish completely upon being lit with no traces of ash.

How does this apply? One of my favorite things to do is to write down all the educational zombie related problems that I have on a piece of flash paper. After doing so, I take a lighter and touch it to one corner and then toss the note away from my body. Within a blink of an eye, the paper (and words that are written on it) vanishes. It is one hundred percent gone without a trace.

I am not so naive to say that all of your problems will just vanish as in my illustration. Although you can take comfort that they will eventually go away. If you apply just a few of the concepts in this book, you will be on a great path to seeing the undead leave your classroom, school, district, and maybe even your state.

One thing that we know will never change in education, is everything is going to change! If there is a new "initiative", educational program, colleague, content standards, or even school principal you just don't care for, take hope in the fact that it will not last forever. The scary thing is just like in a real zombie apocalypse, once you overcome one obstacle it seems that an even more severe problem is waiting for you. Don't let the thought of future problems or past setbacks keep you from fighting the battle at hand. I know it can seem very overwhelming at times!

We all have used the phrase, "I just have so much on my plate!" Do you know the best way to remove "things" from your plate? The first way is to just start eating. Bite by bite! With each bite you take, you are removing problems. The second-best way is to share your "food". You have an alliance, right? Seek out help from others to get some of the problems and aggravations removed.

Again, you will go through each hardship and eventually will overcome them. In doing so you have gained strength. Just like in an actual physical battle, you are now more equipped with that gained strength to fight more problematic foes. In return, don't forget about those who helped you fight. Those alliance members who helped you "clean your plate". Join their fight to help them deal with their educational zombies!

Survival Summary:

- ☣ The current battle you are facing will not last forever.
- ☣ Rest up after a battle because the chances of having to fight another one is strong.
- ☣ Before you can make the negative "disappear" you have to recognize it and be thoughtful in making it go away.
- ☣ Don't let past setbacks or future problems distract from the fight at hand.
- ☣ Don't forget to help others in your alliance fight off their educational zombies!

Dead Discussion:

1. What "light at the end of the tunnel" can you see in your current battle?
2. Is there something you can change today that will make your current battle be over quicker?
3. Rate your current battles in order of importance, are there some battles you can just "stop"?

-Performing First Aid-

It has been five days since there has been an "incident" in your personal sector, located in room 310. Your leader has praised your efforts over the past week. You know he recognizes the difficult time you have had, and it feels good to have a "badge of honor" handed to you. Then you hear something that sets the tiny hairs on the back of your neck on edge. Instinctively, you cover your ears, but turn your head to where you see a little girl screaming while gripping her right hand with her left. Blood pours from the section of flesh that lies between her thumb and index finger. As the red liquid flows from her hand to her elbow, you immediately reach for your communication device. You dial the chief medical officer. The number is input without thinking. As you listen to nothing but steady "rings" you quickly realize there was an announcement this morning stating that all medical personnel would be gone for the day due to receiving additional training at an off-site location. As you drop the phone, you reach for your personal first aid kit and rapidly search for some white gauze. With laser precision and unhuman like speed, you grab the soft bandage, unroll it, and wrap the young girl's hand before any more loss of blood can occur. You look around, to see if any others have been hurt. After a brief moment you glance toward the door to see if the screams attracted any unwanted "zombies". When all imminent danger has passed you address your entire group that you have been assigned to lead for at least the next ten months. "Students, I have told you that when we are doing our cutting and paste activities you have to be very careful. Even though these are "safety scissors" they still will cut you. I also would like to remind you that the school nurse is out today for updated CPR training, so let's try to watch what we are doing for the rest of the day." As you walk the young girl back to her seat you take one final look at the room's entrance. You thought for sure your nosey neighbor in classroom 311 would be coming in to "see what was wrong". It seems like she finds any excuse to make you look bad in front of others. If there were ever an educational zombie, she would be one for sure!

In a world being destroyed by walking corpses-there are going to be limited doctors, few medications, and little medical assistance. In this case, you better learn one thing really quick, first aid! Have you ever heard the phrases, "That person just took a cheap shot at me!" or "You better have a tough chin."? What do those phrases mean? Where do they originate from? The answer is simple, fighting! Taking shots refers to getting literal or figurative punches thrown, whereas having a tough chin means you are able to withstand those punches without being knocked out. If one thing is for certain in your educational zombie apocalypse, it is the fact that you are going to have battles. Your understanding of basic first aid will not only save your life, but it will also save your career!

On Yourself

If one thing is for certain, as the world is ending and turning into a walking graveyard, you are going to get some bites and scratches along with a whole host of other injuries. It is imperative that you are able to do some level of medical repairs on yourself. Your enemies are going to be attacking you from all sides. It does not matter if you have a multitude of vacation time coming up, if you have so many "cuts" that you will bleed to death in the first few days.

The point here is simple. Many things add to making a school year hard. Your bites, cuts, breaks, and bruises can come from lame leadership, pushy parents, tanked test scores, sassy students, critical colleagues, and frustrating faculty meetings. Maybe your hundred-dollar stipend, for five hundred dollars' worth of work, cleared you around sixty-seven bucks after taxes. The promotion that you thought for sure would be awarded to you for your efforts was given to someone else. Whatever the case may be, you have been beaten up by numerous enemies. I have learned that one of the greatest qualities you could possess is the quality of self-encouragement. In these rough times, you better have a lot of "self-encouragement crème" in your first aid kit.

So how does one encourage themselves? The first thing that you need to do, is realize one very simple truth. There are always people who may appear to have it a little better than you, but there are always people who have it much worse. As you start to feel yourself getting overwhelmed with the bites and scratches from the educational undead, keep this in mind. You do not need to look very hard to see other people who are going through tough times. Once you can see beyond your own troubles, and start looking at the troubles of others, you are on the fast track to self-encouragement.

Don't think for a minute that your situation is being downplayed in comparison to others. I will be the first to say that you may have a rowdy group of students, maybe your most recent data makes it appear like you have not taught a single standard, or your supervisor just doesn't seem to remember what it was like to be "in the trenches." I would never say that your troubles are not real and very aggravating, to say the least. I would like to ask you to take a small moment to look around at other people. I am confident you will find some facing situations that are much worse.

For example, there may be other teachers that have groups of students worse than you. Maybe your fellow teacher's data is just a notch above terrible. What if your district is experiencing budget cuts and several faculty members are not having their contracts renewed. Beyond educational related problems, people are being diagnosed with terrible illnesses, losing family members, going through deep depression, or facing crippling financial problems.

Once again, I am not saying you don't know what tough times are like, but many other people have severe things going on as well. When you open your eyes to the complications of others you will start to see that just maybe you have it better than what you originally thought, and with that, you can gain some encouragement.

Building upon the concept that many others have problems in their life too, you need to reflect upon the good things going on in your own life. Even in a time where you feel you are being overrun by the undead, take some moments each day to think upon the people, situations, and things that are happening with you and be thankful for what you have been given.

When you have a thankful heart, you are able to take on the other "enemies" that are trying to overtake you in such a bleak zombie-ridden educational world. Being thankful can be expressed in many ways. One of the best ways to show that you are thankful is with your actions. It is one thing to tell someone, "Hey thanks, I really appreciated you covering my class the other day when I had to leave suddenly." But it is another thing to say, "Hey thanks, I really appreciated you covering my class the other day when I had to leave suddenly. So I swung through the drive-thru this morning and got you this sausage biscuit and coffee." Letting your actions speak for you is the best way to express your thankfulness. You will learn that when you do those kind acts for others, you are doing something internally to yourself. You will feel better, stronger even! You have found a way to bandage up some wounds on your own body so you can be better equipped to bandage up the wounds of others!

On Others

Being able to perform first aid will not only be a benefit when you have to treat your own wounds but you will also be able to treat the wounds of others. You may be thinking, *why would other people be experiencing wounds during MY educational zombie apocalypse?* The answer to that question is simple and clear. As mentioned earlier, if you are experiencing difficult times, there is a good chance those around you are also experiencing hardships. Remember when we talked about self-encouragement, and one way to do that is to meditate about what you have to be thankful for in comparison to those around you. This is an extension of that concept. The fact of the matter is, others will be facing many of the same difficulties that you are having. If you can administer first aid on others who are hurting, you will have a critical part in them being able to overcome their "injuries" which will result in an overall stronger organization.

Do you recall the story of Androcles? I am sure that many of you do but for those few who may be wondering what story I am referring to, I will save you an internet search. Androcles was the man that removed the thorn and bandaged the injured paw of a lion. Later in the story, Androcles and the lion were both captured and imprisoned by an emperor. For sport, Androcles and the lion were forced to go against each other in a pit, which should have resulted in a quick death to poor ole Androcles. The lion however never attacked the man because he remembered the kindness Androcles had shown him. As a result, the emperor pardoned both Androcles and the lion because he saw the bond of friendship that had been developed between man and beast.

Let's apply the Androcles concept to your educational zombie apocalypse. When you are able to relieve the pain and help heal the wounds of others, those actions are not quickly forgotten. What better way to help strengthen your alliance, or to gain a new alliance member, than to help others out in a time of need. As a result of your kindness, you will in return be shown the same kindness. These acts of kindness could include a whole host of things. Covering a duty assignment, buying lunch, purchasing a soft drink, bringing in baked goods, helping with resources, sharing lesson ideas, writing a friendly note, or just offering a pat on the back and smile is just a few things you could do to show kindness.

Please don't take this the wrong way. You should not perform a "first aid" act of kindness on an educational "zombie bite" just to get something back in return. We should be willing to do what is right because it is simply the right thing! But one cannot argue that a great outcome of an act of kindness is returned kindness.

Survival Summary:

- ⊛ You need to be able to "care" for your wounds through self-encouragement.
- ⊛ Rely on your alliance and rest when you can.
- ⊛ When you have reached a good level of health make sure you help others with their "injuries".
- ⊛ The more "healthy" individuals you have in your alliance the stronger your overall organization will be.
- ⊛ You will be rewarded for the acts of kindness you show.

Dead Discussion:

1. What are your most "damaged" areas that need some first aid attention?
2. Are you able to administer first aid on your alliance member's "zombie bites"? How?
3. What are some acts of kindness that you could show? Who in your organization will you show these acts to?

-Good Communication-

    While you were reporting to duty this morning, you came upon a very sneaky "enemy". It was not the typical "zombie" trying to bite at you or the internal enemy waiting for you to make a mistake. It was a different type of enemy...it was the large pothole that has yet to be filled located by your designated parking space. As a result, your car went plunging into what seemed like a deep abyss, two tires on your sport utility vehicle blew out, rendering your mode of transportation useless. As you made your way into the building, you pulled out your cell phone and dialed the number to the vehicle repair headquarters. Upon entering through the main doors, you are explaining to the mechanic, on the other end of the line that you will need to "re-tire" your vehicle. The teacher from room 311 catches only a part of your conversation. Throughout the day you had several staff members ask you how you are feeling and if you are okay. You answer, "Yes", and find it odd that so many would be concerned about two flat tires. At the end of the day one of your fellow alliance members comes up to you and says,

    "I just heard you were going to retire! I don't want you to leave. I know you have had a hard year and all the new academic changes are weighing on your mind. Is it something I have done to make you want to leave?"

    You answer, "Retire! I've not said anything about wanting to retire. I love teaching!" Then it hits you! You remember your conversation earlier with the tire changing service and recall the person who was close by. You realize she was listening to your conversation. You roll your eyes as you think about how this is not the only time "Room 311" has spread damaging rumors based upon miscommunication!

With society collapsing all around, it is critical to keep an open line of communication, not only with your alliance but also with those who may be seeking to bring you harm. Since the beginning of time, humans needing to talk with each other has been an essential part of survival.

Early methods of communication consisted of messenger doves and smoke signals. As advancements were made so did the ease of sharing information. We have evolved from Morse code to the modern-day cellular phone technology. When lines of communication are broken it is much easier to be overtaken by an enemy, whether that enemy be living or in somewhat of a "mixed" living dead state.

Post It

I am the type of person who does not have much of a social media presence at all. Although, I understand there are many positives that can come from the social media platform. I also see the harms it has caused and will continue to cause. I am not going to get into what I believe those downfalls are because to deny the overall popularity of social media would not only be naïve, it would be silly. Even as I sit here writing this book, I admit that I will be using multiple social media platforms to share this information with the rest of the world. My father has always jokingly said, "You better brag on yourself from time to time because not many will do it for you." In today's world with the "dog eat dog" mentality or rather "zombie eat human" this statement has more truth than humor.

Capitalizing on social media is a great way to communicate because it is a platform that reaches more people than anything else. You can share with various stakeholders ranging from your students, parents, to administration staff on what you are accomplishing. Many schools (including the one I lead) posts several bits of information almost daily of all the great things that are happening. This ranges from students climbing on a rock wall in gym class to solving inequalities in sixth-grade math. By doing this you reach a variety of people. The vast majority of those people are NOT the ones trying to tear you from limb to limb.

Those positive connections allow all involved to see and join in the "fight" against the educational zombies. "How do those from the outside help in the battle?" you may ask. They help by *sharing* the good news with others. This helps keep the negative at bay just a little while longer, allowing you just a few more moments to advance in the fight and make headway. These little victories are what will keep you encouraged to do what you know is right. The positive energy that is gained will keep you on a straight path and focused on the big goal!

He Said-She Said

If you have been in any educational role for very long you are well acquainted with the whole "he said-she said" problems. This is when a young person comes to you with a story of a classmate and how that classmate has wronged them. After a thorough investigation of all parties, you quickly learn that there were many omitted details from the original "tattle teller". Now that you have invested entirely too much time on this problem, you have determined that not much can be done because it boils down to the dreaded "he said-she said" dilemma. This is where you could not be able to see the situation any clearer even if you were looking through the Hubble telescope.

Guess what? The same situation will happen with adults! If you are not careful you will have people sharing things about you that is not even close to being accurate. If you do not keep an open line of communication with all stakeholders (inside and outside of your organization) you could create some problems for yourself. I assure you that if you don't tell "your story" someone else will.

If you are doing amazing things in your class then you need to promote that. If your data is off the charts then you need to make sure your students, their parents, and your administrators know it. If you think you are going to have a hard year, and know that your end of year results will be much lower than previous years, let that be known as well. On the other hand, if you feel like you're going to be highly successful, put that comment out for people to hear.

The fact of the matter is, you need to be in control of your communication with others and make sure that communication is clear and free from unwanted "zombie" bias. If you want to keep the educational zombies and other enemies from overtaking you, make sure you have that open line of communication to share what is happening, whether it be good or bad. Remember, sharing the bad allows you to garner support from your trusted alliance. Sharing the good promotes you, your student's, alliance, and organization's success.

You're Breaking Up

We have all been there, you are driving along on a very important call and then all of the sudden the line of communication between you and the person becomes choppy. The words you hear come in short waves and burst. Eventually, all you can hear is silence. What has happened? Your call has been dropped. The line of communication has been broken! You have entered a "dead zone"!

Let's pretend you and one of your actual zombie apocalypse alliance members are searching for much-needed provisions in an old warehouse. You each decide to split up to make the search more efficient, but decide to communicate with two-way radios. Unknown to you, your partner, who is searching the second floor comes across a zombie horde. Somehow, she manages to escape her enemy's clutches injury free. She does not only evade the fearsome bites she actually entraps the zombies in a food storage room. As a good alliance member should, she alerts you quickly! As your radio goes off you hear, "A...lot...of....food....on.....second.....floor....please....go ....there." What you don't realize is that is NOT the message that was intended. The actual message should have been heard as the following: *There is **a lot of** zombies in the **food** storage room **on** the **second floor**. **Please** do not **go** in **there**.* You see, the broken line of communication made a very harmful situation appear promising.

When the communication between various stakeholders is broken or miscommunicated a lot of negative things can start to happen. One of my biggest failures as a first-year principal was in communication. I am not saying I am perfect at it now because that would be a huge overstatement, but I have improved. I never wanted to misrepresent information or not share it with my staff, community, district office or students. Even though I did not have good communication on purpose, the fact of the matter is that it still happened.

You see, one does not have to intend to do something that causes harm to still cause the harm. I wanted to keep a line of communication open, but I missed the mark terribly. How do I know I missed the mark? I was told what seemed like a million times by others of all the things I needed to do differently. Keeping people "in the loop" and not appearing as I was "flying by the seat of my pants" was always in the forefront of those conversations.

As mentioned earlier, I have made strides in that area. One of the main things that I personally have done and would advise others to do is to get a three to five-year calendar planner. Yes, an "old school" physical planner that is about the size of a five-subject notebook. You will learn the longer you are in a specific role that some things will change all the time, but there are a few things that stay fairly consist. This planner will allow you to compare what you did last year to what you need to do this year. It allows you to have a system of consistency from year to year.

As you all know by now there are many things you will need to communicate year after year. These events often occur at about the same time. I take my planner and formulate what I refer to as an "upcoming dates" email. I have used the same email for years now, I just always delete and add new items. In the past, I mapped out about three or four months at a time and would send that to my staff. The things that are listed include picture day, Secret Santa exchange, field trips, common assessments, monthly birthday celebrations, and school-wide assemblies.

Basically, if it is happening at the school it is in the email. Every item does not apply to every single person, but it allows for the entire staff and a few other district office stakeholders to be aware of what is going on in the building. This allows for only a small chance for those real sneaky educational zombies to pick apart not only your flesh but your credibility. Remember what happens when you start to lose your credibility? It is extremely difficult to regain it. This system allows for little room for confusion, because you have been open in your communication. I have given others time to adjust their plans and schedules based upon school wide and district initiatives.

As a teacher you can apply this concept to your classroom. I could see where this would be extremely valuable, especially if you teach older grades. Keeping your students updated and informed well in advance may really benefit you as the teacher. It also will help the parents who you view as a resource ample time to make arrangements to possibly be an assistance for particular events. On the flip side, it allows those who you consider to be an educational zombie or just simply an enemy to be well informed. This may save you from future aggravations.

Broken communication is just as dangerous as no communication. Think back to the example of the two-way radios that was presented moments ago. If your alliance member had told you nothing, more than likely when you approached the second-floor food storage room you would have proceeded with great care, because you always exercise caution in unknown places in a time of the undead uprising. With the broken communication, on the other hand, you received what you thought was to be an accurate message. You may have then allowed yourself to lower your guard because you assumed the food storage room was free from danger, and that you needed to assist in collecting the much-needed supplies. If you want to keep the educational zombies away you can help yourself out tremendously by keeping all lines of communication coming in and going out clear and hopefully positive.

Survival Summary:

- ☣ Communicating your "story" is a vital part of defeating educational zombies.
- ☣ Social media can be a great tool for sharing a vast amount of information in a short period of time with various stakeholders.
- ☣ Keep lines of communication open and clear at all times.
- ☣ Broken or miscommunication can lead to just as many negative consequences as no communication at all!
- ☣ Develop a communication plan that fits the needs of your classroom and organization.

Dead Discussion:

1. Who do you need to communicate with the most?
2. What modes of communication are you currently using?
3. What are some issues you have faced in the past due to miscommunication/lack of communication? (This can be a lack of communication from you or from other sources.)

-A New Beginning-

Ten days have passed since the final encounter. The last battle! Your commanding officer has given orders for all "zombie" response team members to take an approximate ninety-day leave. You are glad to oblige him. You wake up early each morning...old habits are hard to break. As you step outside of your personal living quarters you glance to the east. As a large orange sphere makes its way over the distant hills you close your eyes. The rising sun mixed with a cool June breeze sends chills over your body. Then an evil thought creeps into your mind. You start recalling all the difficult times you have recently had. You think about all the "zombies" and other enemies you have had to face over the past several months. Then you catch the scent of the warm liquid you hold in your left hand. The dark steaming drink has served its purpose as both a vital resource and weapon in days gone by, and it does the same on this perfect morning. As you raise the mug to your lips you dismiss all negative thoughts. You open your eyes to enjoy the morning sunrise. In the back of your mind you know that there are still "zombies" out there somewhere, moving around slowly, seeking something or someone to bite. You don't deny the fact that other enemies, sneakier in nature, are preparing their next ambush. Then a new fragrance enters your nose. As you lower your mug and tilt your head ever so slightly, you listen hard and can hear a "sizzle" sound coming from inside. The smell and the sound combined remove any of those small traces of negativity. You think to yourself, "There will always be troubles, but today is a new day, today is the eleventh day of summer break, and by the smell of it, my spouse is up fixing us bacon!"

The best part of a dark storm cloud is that there is a silver lining. That silver lining lets us know that a fresh start is coming…a new beginning. The greatest part of a new beginning is that you have a clean slate.

Every single person will experience times of trials and distress. Some will have extensive periods when they feel the weight of the looming "apocalypse" push them to new depths. Others will maybe only have short burst of difficult times. No matter the length of the battle, the fact still remains, it can be a very depressing and lonely endeavor.

As I have mentioned before, you can take HOPE in the fact that the battles you face will not last forever. As a result of all the educational undead zombies and human form enemies being eliminated or at least in a far-off location, you need to reset.

The field of education is a very unique profession. There are a lot of factors that are out of our control, no matter what role you are in. There are times where educational professionals are viewed as less than what they really are. This should not be the case! Educators play a critical role in society and should be looked at with great respect. Like all professions there have been those who have "tainted" the pool by making very poor decisions. It is up to the rest of us to make up for those few times educators failed to serve the correct purpose.

When you apply the various chapters of this book together as a collective whole the outcome will be amazing! If you allow yourself to focus on overcoming the multiple educational zombies, human enemies, and limited resources you will be able to stay on course! You will be able to build an alliance, collect weapons for survival, and have opportunities for rest!

So again, I say, the best part of the dark storm clouds is the small silver lining that surrounds the edges. It is there as a symbol of hope. The fighting is over and a new day, a new beginning, is upon us!

Glossary

Listed below you will find some basic terms that are used throughout the book. Each term has a brief "personal definition" of how it relates to an actual zombie apocalypse and how it relates to an educational zombie apocalypse.

Alliance

- Zombie-A trusted group of fellow humans that have a unique skill set that compliments your own abilities. All those in the group have a common goal in mind...to survive and search for a cure that will result in a better quality of life.

- Educational-A trusted group of fellow teachers, friends, coaches, administrators, etc. that have a unique skill set that compliments your own abilities. You each have a common goal to move forward in education and see your students be successful.

Apocalypse

- Zombie-A time when humans have undergone a massive biological change. Upon exposure to a virus through a zombie bite or upon death, living humans now become undead enemies.

- Educational-A time in your educational career where you feel that you are fighting daily to survive. It seems you have trouble awaiting you around every corner and your educational world seems to be falling apart.

Bite

- Zombie-When a zombie gnashes down on a victim with their teeth. The attack results in the human victim "turning" into a zombie because the bite leads to a quick death due to the rapid spread of the infectious disease.

- Educational- Any "attack" that a teacher may experience. For example, multiple site visits with no meaningful feedback, negative criticism from coworkers, regulation changes, job description change, etc. If you are not properly armored (being positive, having a good alliance and support system, housed in a gated community") the "bite" will eventually meet flesh and you too will "turn".

Cure

- Zombie-An antidote that when taken prevents you from turning into a zombie upon death or from a zombie bite.

- Educational-A positive attitude that will allow you to overcome all the attacks you get from various educational zombies.

Corner Post

- Zombie-A strong post, set at the corner of your fence where your fence turns. This allows you to encircle your entire community. The corner post is in line with your focal point.

- Educational-The point in which you reached your goal. A time to celebrate, but also a time to make a turn into a new direction and find a new goal to achieve.

Focal Point

- Zombie-An immovable object off in the distance (tree, large rock, or even another architectural structure) that serves as a guide when you are building a fence for your "gated community". The object allows you to maintain focus and stay on course.

- Educational-The main goal you are trying to achieve. The big picture. As long as you keep that goal in mind you continue to stay on a good straight path to success.

Gated Community

- Zombie-A place of safety for an organized group and/or alliance. Surrounded by some type of structure, such as a fence or wall to prevent zombies and other enemies from entering.

- Educational-A safe place for educators to share thoughts, ideas, and concerns with their alliance (mentor teachers, peers, coaches) without the fear of being criticized or subjected to negativity.

Living Enemies

- Zombie-The living humans that use this time of chaos for their own benefit. They seek to harm others, do whatever they must to advance, loot/steal, etc. They do not look out for others in their alliance, they are selfish by nature.

- Educational-Sadly enough not much different than the "zombie definition for living enemies". These are mainly the internal enemies that are often more manipulative and seek to destroy others around them, that they may survive themselves. These enemies often have unmet professional/personal needs and secretly despise those who are moving forward as a collective group.

Resources

- Zombie-Food, water, shelter, weapons, medical supplies, fuel, modes of transportation, tools, etc.

- Educational-support staff, infrastructure, textbooks, materials, grants (other free related items), volunteers, guest speakers, etc...and of course COFFEE!

Turn

- Zombie-The change that occurs in a human after they are bitten by a zombie or upon death as result of a dormant virus that lives inside each human. The victim then joins the zombie mob.

- Educational-The change that occurs in an educator's life after exposure to an educational zombie bite. The change results in decreased motivation, an increase in negative behavior, and an overall lack of concern for their job.

Weapons

- Zombie-gun, knife, hammer, ninja throwing star, sword, bow staff, nunchaku, sai, etc. (I never miss an opportunity for a good Teenage Mutant Ninja Turtle reference).

- Educational-Technology, classroom management, relationship building, engagement and understanding the mind of your "enemy".

Zombie, Living Dead, Biter, Undead, Animated Corpse, Etc.

- Zombie-A human that has been infected by a deadly virus causing them to "turn" upon death into a monstrous flesh eater. The human body now is in an "undead" state and serves as a host for the virus. It can only be defeated with a vital blow to the brain.

- Educational-Many of the enemies that we face in education such as standardized testing, poor funding, discipline problems, weak leadership, limited resources, etc. These enemies can be both external and internal. It is very important to understand the mind and attack the brain of this enemy.

-Author's Notes-

As we end this journey together, I would like to share a few things about myself. My name is Woody Underwood and I have been married to my high school sweetheart, Elizabeth (Britt) Underwood since 2003. I have two of the most wonderful children named Woodrow Carson and Emma Jayde.

Early in my career I taught at Garrison Elementary School for five years as the P.E. and health teacher. I then was blessed to serve as the assistant principal at the same elementary school as well as Lewis County High School for one year. In 2013 I took on the challenge of running for a public office in my county and was elected in 2014. I am currently at the beginning of my second term in that elected officials' role.

In 2014 I was offered a principal's position at Tollesboro Elementary School in Lewis County, Kentucky. I graciously accepted! Being in leadership roles for a large portion of my life has been a very eye-opening experience. I am humbled daily by the blessings that have been bestowed upon me, and in return I would like to be a blessing to others.

I would like to say once again that I currently, never have, nor never will believe in an actual zombie apocalypse. Although, I love sci-fi movies and books and found the correlation between the difficult times in education and an undead takeover to be not only a bit humorous but accurate. As mentioned at the beginning of this book my passion for leading and teaching young people is great. That passion is also mixed with a deep desire to be an encouragement to others, especially when they are going through hard times. I have been blessed to work with amazing people in my career, but I have gained great insights into other organizations through collaboration and "alliance building". I know the struggles that are discussed throughout this book are real and impact many of those in education today.

I have a great fear that if things don't change collectively for the better, education will be facing serious battles in the future. With that being said I understand that collective change will not occur until there are individual changes in the lives of people. It is hard to get up every day knowing that so many problems are facing you, and many of those problems occur before you ever step foot inside your organization's building. You must find some solace in your ability to deal with these problems.

I am not so arrogant to think that the insights I have provided are foreign to you. Remember the second thing I learned about being a principal? I learned that I could not "pull the wool" over the eyes or "fool" my staff. I would not intend to do the same to you. My goal for this book is to apply basic and practical advice based upon my life's experiences to hopefully help, encourage, and support others in their daily educational zombie battles. If you are having a difficult time in education, do your very best to, *TEACH LIKE IT'S THE ZOMBIE APOCALYPSE!*